Spirituality of the New Testament

Cross and Crown Series of Spirituality

LITERARY EDITOR

Reverend Jordan Aumann, O.P., S.T.D.

NUMBER 19

GUSTATE ET VIDETE

Spirituality
of the
New Testament

W. K. GROSSOUW

translated by MARTIN W. SCHOENBERG, O.S.C.

B. HERDER Book Co.

15 & 17 South Broadway, St. Louis 2, Mo.
AND 2/3 Doughty Mews, London, W.C.1

A translation of *Bijbelse Vroomheid, Beschouwingen over de spiritualiteit van het Nieuwe Testament,* by W. K. Grossouw, published by Uitgeverij het Spectrum, Utrecht/Antwerp, Fifth Edition, 1959.

NIHIL OBSTAT:

Aloysius J. Mehr, O.S.C., J.C.D.
Censor Librorum

IMPRIMI POTEST:

Very Rev. Benno Mischke, O.S.C.
Provincial

IMPRIMATUR:

✠ Leo A. Pursley, D.D.
Bishop of Fort Wayne—South Bend
March 2, 1961

© Copyright 1961 by B. Herder Book Co.
Library of Congress Catalog Card Number: 61-12285
Printed in the U.S.A.

Translator's Preface

IT WOULD BE PLEASANT to present this translation as being all my own; but it would not be true. Without the help of my confreres and my students at the Crosier House of Studies, it would have been simply impossible to do it at all.

Therefore my grateful acknowledgment and my sincerest appreciation to all of them, but especially to Father van Roosmalen for patiently checking the translation against his own native tongue of the original, to Frater Ronald Kidd for reading and correcting the translation for its English, and to Frater Joseph Sullivan for supervising the processing of the manuscript.

Since the original was first given in the form of conferences to students at the Catholic University of Nijmegen (Holland), and the author is himself a master of both his subject and his language, I have tried always to keep in mind the college student or his equivalent in making this translation.

MARTIN SCHOENBERG, O.S.C.

v

Author's Foreword

THESE SKETCHES are intended as an effort (in union with many others) toward rendering the inexhaustible treasures of the Bible more readily accessible to the Catholics of our day. It would be unquestionably much better to read the sacred text itself. Julien Green wrote in his *Journal* under the date of February 14, 1942: "It is the Bible alone which is eternally young, like a mountain stream cascading into the depths for thousands of years. It is not only the most youthful of all books, but the most recent as well, and the most actual. Whatever shall be written has been written in it. The writer of a thousand years from now is even now antiquated when compared with the Bible."

Nonetheless, a great many Catholics never get around to reading the Sacred Scriptures unless they are first shown in some more or less "practical" manner what the Bible can mean for their personal lives. The task of this book therefore is to outline in simple fashion the existential values of the New Testament. It is consequently not scientific in the commonly accepted sense of the term, although it did originate in conferences given to the students at the Catholic University of Nijmegen. The intense and profound reaction witnessed there have confirmed a long-standing conviction that the men of today, no less than the men of the past, hunger more for the word of God than for bread.

W. G.

Contents

x Contents

PART THREE

The Gospel of St. John

Spirituality of the New Testament

Introduction

CATHOLICISM IN OUR TIMES evidences growing appreciation and awareness of the Bible. At the same time it is clear that the Scriptures still are not of sufficiently vivid concern to our Catholic people, whether clerical or lay. The soaring sales, however, especially of pocket-editions of the New Testament, are a gratifying token of a renewed interest in the holy book. Bible groups or study clubs, especially among young adults, exist in various locales and in highly divergent situations. In some families even, the father himself reads a portion of the Scriptures at table.

Most commonly and rightly the Catholic encounters the Bible in the liturgy. But here we stumble upon a kind of vicious circle. Liturgists commonly complain that public worship, especially the liturgy of the word, is too little known, too far removed from the ordinary believer, and for many reasons does not occupy its rightful place. One of the conditions to be fulfilled if the liturgy is to be grasped and experienced personally is precisely that the Scriptures be known and appreciated. And one of the obstacles to the fruitful realization of the Fore-Mass is the commonly unbiblical character of the sermon. This in turn means that the spiritual life of many priests has scant grounding in the Bible, if indeed any at all.

For the birth and growth of a living Catholicism, not merely resting on the past but open to the future, love for the Scriptures must needs increase in intensity and currency. This is particularly necessary at the present time for the following reasons. In the first place there is the intimate bond with the liturgy to which reference has already been made. It is impossible to take a truly active part in the liturgy of the word without penetrating into the letter and spirit of the Bible. No matter what sort of reform in the liturgy may be imminent, it is certain that the Scriptures will continue to supply the major portion of the texts for public worship. But it is also certain that the instructed Catholic of this age will no longer permit himself to be pacified with a passive "attendance in good behavior"; he spontaneously longs for an *actuosa participatio,* an active participation in worship. The ideal, prophetically anticipated and clearly outlined by the saintly Pius X, is now in common possession, spontaneous and obvious to all who are concerned about worship. This situation accords with the *Zeitgeist* of our world, which is democratic, striving to see all people come of age in freedom and self-realization, and grappling for the preservation of basic values. The believer wants to know what is going on, to understand what is being said, to participate in those events which are also *his* doing. He realizes that what takes place in the Sunday Mass is more meaningful than afternoon devotions or the rosary.[1]

For an intimate participation in the liturgy it is certainly not necessary that it become transparent in its entirety or in every constituent part. There will always remain, and there must always remain, a certain numinous penumbra which can be approached only by faith. The mystery proper is not comprehended, but only encountered and experienced. However, large portions of the lit-

---

[1] Father Doncoeur, S.J., asserted at a liturgical congress: "When the psalms of the Office had become a dead letter for the people, they discovered the rosary. When the Eucharistic offering had become a dead cult for the people, in which they could participate neither with words, song, nor rite, they discovered the processions, the shrines, and the afternoon devotions. Now that the tenor of the times no longer teaches the great mysteries of faith and redemption to the layman, he is discovering the months of Mary and of the poor souls in purgatory" (from the original French in *Voor een levende Liturgie,* Universitas-Schriften, 4, p. 90).

urgy, and especially the Fore-Mass, expressly mean to teach and instruct. Further, the believer of our day wants to comprehend what can reasonably be understood. But how is this possible without a knowledge of the Scriptures, and how will this knowledge be available without a preaching that is saturated with the biblical spirit?

Knowledge and love of the Bible cannot be dispensed with for the added reason that through the Scriptures we stand midstream in the great and undying tradition of the Christianity of all centuries. As Catholics we know neither our own roots nor our ground if we do not know the Scriptures. Where so many forms and expressions of devotion are caught up in the transitory, and particularly in our time where traditional institutions are falling apart, tossed about in subjection to destructive criticism, it is more necessary than ever to preserve and love the essential nucleus. It is not without reason that in our day we hear time and again the invitation to return to the sources, even in the matter of religious instruction and spiritual life. The foremost source of our Christian spirituality is the Bible. The nucleus of our Catholic piety has been borne and is still being borne by God's own word in the Scriptures. One need only think for a moment of the Gospels, the epistles of Paul, and the psalms as the centuries-old prayer of the synagogue and Church, to realize that the true treasures of our spiritual life are to be found there. Throughout all centuries the saints and doctors of the Church, as also her priests and religious, and even the so-called ordinary faithful have drawn light and strength from this source. The Bible has wielded a great influence in forming Catholic tradition and the concrete shape of the Christian life. A man cannot be Catholic without standing in its light and living under its power, even though he may not be aware of this. If he wishes to perceive his own Catholic character, if he wishes to be a cognizant and convinced Christian, a certain knowledge and appreciation of the Bible is simply indispensable.

All this is necessary for still another reason. Throughout all Christendom today there is an intense longing for unity. This longing will be satisfied by nothing less than the fulfillment of the precept and prayer of the Lord and Savior: that all be one. In spite of separation and division, we are united with all non-Catholic Christians not only by faith in the same Lord but also by belief in the same Bible as the word of God. There we find a common source of dialogue, given us by the Spirit himself. In praying the Our Father and Christ's high-priestly prayer we are on common ground. Unfortunately, even on this point unity is threatened and thwarted by all manner of divergency in interpreting the one word of God. The obstinacy and subtlety of theologians pertain to the most apparent consequences of original sin and have in the course of centuries frightened many a simple soul from studying this most exalted of all sciences and even from belief in the divine revelation. Granted that scientific exegesis is indispensable, yet it is not scientific exegesis which entrenches the word of God unalterably in our human world. The Catholic believes that when all is said and done, the Bible is preserved inviolate only within the sacred confines of the Church and under the tutelage of her teaching authority. However, it ought to be possible for all true Christians to begin with this written word of God in learning to know each other better and in approaching each other with love.

This is certain: many Protestants arrive at a proper estimation of the Catholic Church only with great difficulty because they think that they cannot find the word of God there at all or at best only in a mutilated condition. Most Catholics are scarcely capable of imagining what the Bible means to a Protestant. "The Protestant knows his Bible by heart (*par cœur*), he knows it with his heart through love. There is a bond of affection between him and *his* Bible. It is part and parcel of himself because of his intense love for it. Whenever a Catholic reads the Bible he reads merely *the* Bible, but not *his* Bible. Generally he does not read it at all." [2]

The objection raised by Christians of the Reform to the effect that the Catholic does not have a personal relationship to the

[2] Julien Green, *Journal*, November 5, 1947.

Bible is, unfortunately, well-founded in too many instances. On the other hand, it is also true that the Protestant generally does not sufficiently realize how intimately the Bible is entwined with the Roman liturgy. But the truth of this intimate connection between Scripture and worship comes into its totality only when the liturgy is lived in personal existence. Since this is often entirely wanting, one must conclude that many Catholics neither know nor appreciate the Scriptures, at least not in a manner meaningful for their personal spiritual lives. This void is one of the greatest obstacles toward their being understood by their fellow-Christians of the Reform. As soon as the word of God will become better known and loved among our own people, the truth and the holiness of the Church will not only shine forth more brilliantly, but the reunion of Christians will also be advanced.

Finally, we are experiencing a crisis in spirituality.[3] This crisis manifests itself most patently in what may be called the unconventional and less traditional strata of society, among the intellectuals, among laborers, and generally among the young. The difficulty is occasioned by an externalization of our religion still strongly bearing the characteristics of a phase of society that is past, while our warlike and industrial era is marked by an evolution that is developing so quickly and so radically that one ought rather to look at it as a revolution. It is readily intelligible how certain groups, especially laborers and the young, who have the

[3] The word "spirituality" is an expression which is vague, but in vogue. For this reason it is a convenient term and practically unavoidable. It is not our purpose to enter here into a discussion attempting to give the term a sharply defined sense. One might paraphrase (Christian) spirituality as the attitude of the spirit, the spiritual life, which is characteristic of every Christian, providing the term "spirit" is not taken to mean immaterial, but the essence that inspires a person or a life. For this reason the notion of spirituality is here made to include not one's interior life alone (although it embodies this as its primary constituent element) but the whole concrete activity of the Christian in his spiritual-corporeal unity, comprising his existence in the world and his association with others, so far as this is imbued with an authentic Christian spirit. Hence, in this book dealing with New Testament spirituality, there will be considerations on prayer as also on fraternal charity and matters of Christian morals.

least connection with the past, or artists and intellectuals, who are more sensitive to the signs of the times and the portents of the future, feel this crisis most vehemently, or, to put it in different terms, are the most critical of certain forms and embodiments of Christianity which they consider antiquated.

All these things must naturally be taken with a grain of salt. On the one hand, there is no question here of a sort of crusade to be led against certain types of bourgeois practices. Nothing is gained by being negative, for what has been worn threadbare will not perdure. "That which is obsolete and has grown old is near its end," says the author of Hebrews (8:13). Besides, Christendom is not some abstract essence which can be crystallized into one or another chemically pure state. It is always incarnated, to use a current expression. It cannot exist without all kinds of shapes, exercises, customs, which necessarily share in the character of a particular age. People always experience their religion in a concrete manner, and only in a concrete manner. There is a danger that the intellectual will cherish as religion an abstract fantasy lacking sufficient engagement with reality and the "impure" but living concrete without which a man, because of his corporeal being and social structure, cannot experience his religion. And on the other hand, it is certain that an active form of worship more in accord with the demands of our time is gradually gaining place. For example, wherever serious efforts are being made to celebrate the Sunday Mass in the spirit of the liturgy, the annoying traces of the bourgeois mentality vanish automatically.

All this does not make light of the fact that the fast tempo of our times demands a fast adaptation. Christendom must prove itself to belong to our age also; this is no longer accepted as self-evident. The crisis in which our spirituality finds itself need not degenerate into a catastrophe. It can be the symptom that presages an intense and happy growth. The same people who are so critical of many expressions and forms of Christianity (and whose criticism is vivid proof that religion by no means leaves them indifferent) often manifest a lively concern for the Bible, for the liturgy, for the apostolic witness, in short, for values which have always been essential in Christendom. These interests must be fulfilled, these efforts must be furthered for the sake of man and for the sake of the Church.

There has risen among laborers and intellectuals above all, but also quite naturally among others, an undefined uneasiness in the face of the sensibility which very often still appears to inspire certain pious practices and forms of our religion. This sensuousness is felt to be something complacent, individualistic, moralizing, sentimental, and nervous—something too intimately bound to a certain phase of our society which belongs to the past. It expresses itself in the formulas of prayers, in the "dressing up" of some of our churches, in religious ornamentation, in the instructions to which children must often submit in the schools, in devotional and spiritual literature, and so on. The very abundance of pious practices and devotions can also result in a certain satiety which can obstruct authentic religious commitment. Granted, one may not simply throw overboard the religious heritage of Catholicism; each one does possess the right and liberty to experience his own personal devotion in his own personal way, as long as he submits himself to the guiding hand of ecclesiastical authority. But each one likewise has the liberty, in whatever is free and not obligatory, to strive after sobriety and to restrict himself to essentials. Our time is striving for the profound and simple, for a definite grounding of religion in the essential and primary, not because of laziness, but because we, men of our particular age, have been hurt too painfully in all which is luxury and ornament, and this wound lies deep in the center of our human condition. The words of Dante, "You have the Old and the New Testament, and the pastor of the Church who is guiding you; let these suffice for your salvation," could have been written expressly for us.

The Bible is our salvation in this crisis of religious sensibility and renders it fruitful for the future. It is the classic book of Christianity, in no wise subject to changes of taste and sensitivity. It is part and parcel of every true Christian devotion in every Christian century, each one having drawn inspiration from it. The Scriptures possess a particular universal inclusiveness: whoever is sad or despairs, whoever is joyful or grateful, whoever is lonesome, whoever feels a close tie with all God's children—all find in the Bible words singing with an accent of unmistakable authenticity which fit his mood and situation. In this ancient book all life moves and sparkles; the whole man with his weakness and sin, with repentance and conversion, with his banality and his holiness. The Bible is ripe and grown to maturity. If it had not been such from the beginning, it would have become so through the tears and blood of countless Christian generations. It is masculine, entirely unsentimental, yet loving and tender. If a man thinks he cannot pray, let him reach for the psalms; he will discover that no better prayers exist than these old poems wherein authentic feeling honestly cries out in the presence of God. The spirituality of the Bible is not vapid nor staid. It is pungent and directed toward essentials. It is authentic and in a certain sense removed from all time. It bears the living commitment of all ages.

For all these reasons the Scriptures are extremely helpful in leading the Christian to maturity. Our religious experience must grow from both the rational and the affective, if it is not to languish and even die. What we perceive to be true in the spiritual life of our time as a whole, we see reflected in the spiritual crisis of many individuals. Those who experience a religious dilemma in their decisive years are by far not the worst off, for this proves that their devotional life, too, aspires to leave behind its childhood stage and that they will not grow up into that spiritual monstrosity which our staid, provincial Catholicism often produces in all ranks and classes: the man who is adult in every respect but a puerile dwarf in what pertains to religion, who is happy in this state and even goes so far as to call it childlike docility. But this individual crisis is frequently aggravated unnecessarily through the posture of an unintelligent and nervous milieu which, blind to the long range, sees only the present and desires to hold fast to the traditional devotional practices without mutation or interruption. How greatly man fails the long-suffering of God! Whenever a human being begins to arrive at spiritual maturity, a long process (especially at the present time) is inaugurated, in which the good seed and the weeds grow up simultaneously, in which others are asked only for patience and a love which will not intervene prematurely, which will never "interfere" because of its respect for the maturing personality. Happy the man who from youth has learned to read the Bible as *his* book and to recognize it as the holy ground where he meets God and God speaks to him. *Docuisti me a juventute mea* (Thou hast taught me from my youth). "The Scriptures grow with their readers," says Gregory the Great. "They are not so difficult that they frighten, nor yet so artless that they become banal" (*Moralia,* 20, 1, 1).

In what follows, an effort is made to construct Christian spirituality on some leading themes of the New Testament, or —to express the same thing more modestly and correctly—to ask the New Testament for a few clear directives which must lead a Christian along his path through life. This is only one of the ways in which we can make the Bible fruitful for ourselves. It need not be added that there is no thought whatever of being complete. The Old Testament is left aside on the whole (although because of its rich humaneness it certainly has much to tell our generation), and of the New Testament only a few leading notions will be analyzed and explained in the light of our times. Each age has the obligation of re-interpreting for itself the Scriptures, since they are ever ancient, ever new. Though it may appear superfluous, let it nonetheless be expressly stated that Catholic teaching on the spiritual life is based, or ought to be based, on the Scriptures alone. We are only following in the footsteps of our fathers in the faith when we turn to the Bible for light: "Thy word, O Lord, stands firm forever. . . . Thy word is a lamp to my feet, and a light to my path" (Ps. 118:89, 105).

The division of the matter into three parts is suggested by the threefold division of the leading writings of the New Testament: the direct report of Jesus' words in the so-called Synoptic Gospels (Matthew, Mark, and Luke), the authoritative interpretation of this teaching as it is inspired by the Spirit of God and recorded

in the epistles of Paul and the Gospel of John. The occasional
repetitions which this division entails will be abundantly com-
pensated by the added light which these different approaches will
cast on some of the leading themes of Christian teaching, for
instance, on brotherly love.

PART ONE

The Synoptic Gospels

ONE

The Father in Heaven

THE IMAGE WE FORM of God is a determining factor in the worship we offer Him. The first question we therefore pose for ourselves in studying Christian spirituality is: What did Jesus reveal to us concerning His Father and His relationship to man? The answer is found in the words of the Lord Himself as they are recorded in the three oldest Gospels, those according to Matthew, Mark, and Luke.

Our notion of God has its roots in a soil of varying texture; these roots run deeper than our consciousness. It is possible, and perhaps quite probable, that early impressions of our father's character and the experiences of our youth have left their traces in the picture we have of God. It is also possible that the catechetical instruction and religious formation we received were one-sided and evoked in our childish minds an image of God that aroused fear; an image we would just as soon escape and forget. Then, perhaps, as we grew to adulthood and "put away the things of a child" (I Cor. 13:12), we cast aside—and rightly so!—this childish picture and gave preference to our own selves, ignoring a God who could only angrily impose Himself between us and the ravishingly beautiful creatures about us. How important is the gradual and cautious forming of a correct idea of God! The clear and inexhaustible source for such a notion is to be found in the Gospels.

There Jesus reveals God to man as "their Father who is in

heaven," which is to say, as One who is infinitely beyond men and their world but *at once* their good and considerate Father. God is Lord and God is Father, and both in one.

If we may present the matter in a somewhat simplified manner, we might say that the notion of God as the sole Master and Creator of heaven and earth is borrowed by Jesus from the Old Testament and then continued and developed by Him. It was not unfamiliar for the upright Jew; pure monotheism, the doctrine of the one personal God, Creator and King of all that exists, was precisely what distinguished him in his religious vision from his pagan neighbors. The revelation that came through Jesus has its root in the word which God had spoken earlier through the prophets and the sages (Heb. 1:1). There is no break between the Old and the New Testament, but a continuity established by God Himself. The thought that God is Father of mankind was not entirely new to the Jews, nor even to the pagans, but its first revelation in all its wonder and certitude came through Jesus, *the Son,* because only through Him was kinship with God made possible.

Before we come to a more specific analysis, it is well to dwell momentarily on those ideas which form the nucleus of the New Testament image of God, on the concepts of God's exaltedness and His nearness: God is above all and God is with all. It is precisely the simultaneity of these two characteristics which give the Christian idea of God its dynamism and originality. The *Te Deum* expresses this beautifully when it says: *"Patrem immensae majestatis—Father* of infinite majesty." Both aspects must be preserved and hold each other properly balanced if our reflections on God are not to become distorted. If we emphasize only God's exalted nature there arises a danger to which later Judaism succumbed [1] and which was not always avoided even in Christian

_____

[1] The oft recurring notion among Christians that the Old Covenant is the "law of fear" is not correct. The well-known text: "The fear of the Lord is the beginning of wisdom" (Ps. 110:10, etc.), ought to be translated: Piety is the beginning of wisdom, or preferably, is the best wisdom. The Old Testament does indeed put more emphasis on the awe-inspiring majesty of God; but this emphasis is not one-sided, as may be seen, for example, in Exod. 20:5, 6; 34:6, 7; Ps. 102:8; Joel 2:13.

times: of depicting God as a capricious and erratic tyrant, whose majesty is appalling, if not frightening. Where feeling for the divine holiness is wanting, a different distortion to which Catholics succumb from time to time enters the picture: the danger of nonchalance and a familiarity lacking reverence. (Let it be noted that familiarity in the *proper* sense is a direct result of the Incarnation.)

In the first place, then, Christ proclaimed the *sovereignty* of God. The general picture of His synoptic preaching is that in close adherence to the Old Testament tradition He discreetly but firmly stressed the divine exaltedness while at the same time He brought it close to man and made it bearable by the concomitant teaching of God's fatherhood. Jesus' proclamation of God's majesty was discreet because, to use the common expression, the thunder-and-lightning terminology clothing the appearances of God in the Old Testament is absent. Likewise are missing the epithets of God's dreadfulness which appear so often in the Old Testament (Exod. 15:11; Deut. 7:21, etc.). Even the anthropomorphism of "God's anger," which occasionally crops up in John and Paul, though in a non-emotional sense, is not heard from Jesus' lips. And yet the Master did give strong expression to the incomparable majesty of God, to His transcendent existence. He did this calmly and without clamor as though it were a self-evident truth, a basic phenomenon of a genuine experience of the divine.

A typical text is that of Mark 10:18 (Luke 18:19). To the courageous but somewhat shallow enthusiasm of the rich young man who had addressed Jesus as the "good Master," our Lord reacts with a casual, almost cool reference to the unfathomable abyss which the youth had uncovered with his question on eternal life. "Why dost thou call Me good? No one is good but God only." [2]

A similar spirit pervades that other sentence: "Therefore, if you, evil as you are, know how to give good gifts to your children,

[2] The text of Matt. 19:17, "Why dost thou ask Me about what is good? One there is who is good," is an evident softening of a hard saying which had quickly become unpalatable to Christians because it seemed to exclude Jesus Himself from "goodness."

how much more will your Father in heaven give good things to those who ask Him!" (Matt. 7:11.) The imputation, "evil as you are," is addressed to all listeners without distinction, to all men of all times. God is so good that all others are bad. The language spoken by our Lord here on earth lacked such abstract and philosophical terms as infinite perfection and divine transcendency. Jesus expresses this more simply but also more strikingly, in a concrete way which is applicable to an existent situation and not as a theoretical paradigm. A similar overpowering perception of God's majesty is to be found in Jesus' words on the kingship or sovereignty of God, which will be the subject of the next chapter.

According to the Gospels, the most usual manner in which Jesus expresses God's exaltedness is found in the formula which is common particularly in Matthew: the Father in heaven, or the heavenly Father (the last only in Matthew). These naturally have their origin in an imagery of space. According to the primitive notions of the ancients about the universe, the "All-high" was conceived as dwelling in the heavens, or preferably even in the heaven of heavens, above the earth, above light, and the lower celestial spheres. Heaven is the dwelling and the throne of God. "God is in heaven and you are on earth," says Ecclesiastes (5:1) in his attempt to exhort man to modesty. And the Psalmist adds: "Heaven is the heaven of the Lord, but the earth He has given to the children of men" (113:16). Yet in the Gospels the connotation of locale has been weakened and removed from the focal point, as can be noted from the variant "heavenly Father," which signifies quality rather than place. In the last analysis both expressions have the same meaning and express negatively that God is not earthly, not like man, not bound by the limitations of this earthly existence. Positively they signify God's power and governance of all that happens on earth: [3] it is from heaven that God surveys the earth. "His eyes behold, His eyelids probe the children of men" (Ps. 10:5). That this meaning is also in continuity with the Gospel expression is apparent from the parallel formulas

[3] And also in the "lower heavens." Cf. the petition of the Our Father: Thy will be done on earth *as it is in heaven.*

appearing in the Sermon on the Mount: "And thy Father, who sees in secret, will reward thee" (Matt. 6:4, 6, 18), and: "Your Father knows what you need" (6:8, 32). But according to the preaching of Jesus, God is a Father who has tender care before He is a judge who judges and punishes. He is the Father "who makes His sun to rise on the good and the evil, and sends rain on the just and the unjust" (Matt. 5:45) and is concerned with the welfare of even the least among creatures (Matt 10:29).

One may therefore say that these expressions actually indicate God's transcendency, to use modern terminology, but they do not denote God as the "Unmoved Mover," who has withdrawn himself from the world of man. The Father in heaven bends toward the earth. Men and all human activity are guided by His providence. This balanced description of God's majesty and sovereignty is deprived of all unreality, distance, and cool remoteness precisely by the fact that in the Gospels the words "who is in heaven" are connected by preference with the name "Father."

For the name "Father" is the proper name wherewith according to the Gospels the Master designates God. In this manner He Himself addressed God in all simplicity as "Father," in His own idiom "Abba," a word which, because of its unique ring and its irreplaceable associations, was preserved by the Greek-speaking Christian community (cf. Mark 14:36; Rom. 8:15; Gal. 4:6). He calls God "My Father." But God is also the Father of man. Jesus commands His disciples: "In this manner therefore shall you pray: Our Father who art in heaven . . ." (Matt. 6:9), and repeatedly He tells them: "Your Father who is in heaven," and: "If you do not forgive men, neither will your heavenly Father forgive you your offenses" (Matt. 6:15), and so on in many texts. It has become a platitude to say that Christendom introduced the notion of God's Fatherhood. But one must be careful here of unjustifiable oversimplification. On the one hand, Christians are not alone in calling God "Father"; on the other, it is true that this notion has become complete human reality only in Christendom. (Furthermore, here on earth only faith can approach this reality.)

Even Hellenistic paganism contemporary with Jesus was not entirely unacquainted with the notion of God as Father. From ancient times Zeus had been called "the father of god and men." But this idea is especially prominent in the Stoa,—that grave, moral, and widespread philosophy contemporary with New Testament times—and appears in a form much more spiritual than is to be found in ancient polytheistic paganism. Perhaps it is found in its most beautiful form in the renowned hymn of Cleanthes (3rd century B.C.): "O supremely bountiful Zeus, lord of dark clouds and flashing lightning, be merciful to us, the children of men. Remove, O Father, also the darkness of foolishness from our souls. Grant us insight and right intention as your royal heritage." Diodorous of Siclus (1st century B.C.) renders the idea well with the words: "God is called 'father' because of his solicitude and benevolence toward all, but also because he represents himself to us as the guide of the human race" (V, 72, 2). The slave-sage Epictetus, who lived a little later than Paul, is reported by Arrianus to have taught that "everyone who has contemplated the order of the universe . . . and has become aware that only rational creatures can by their nature hold intercourse with God since they are united to Him by reason—why should such a one not call himself a member of the world community? Why not 'son of God'? And why should he fear anything that can happen among men? Is it possible that kinship to the emperor should give one a sense of security, resistance to contempt and fear,—and yet shall the possession of God as our creator, father, and protector, not be enough to free us from pain and anguish?"[4]

These are exalted thoughts and belong to the summit of paganism. One may surmise that a true religious proclivity, such as was undoubtedly possessed by Cleanthes and Epictetus, enabled them to penetrate intuitively further into this sphere than their

---

[4] I, 9, 4 ff. However, one must read the whole text to see that this divine filiation resolves itself in a genuine Stoic autonomy and autarchy which "relies exclusively on itself" and has no need of anyone else. Both the similarity and difference it has with Matt. 6:25–34 is very instructive.

premises allowed.[5] It is not surprising that similar words could be introduced with approval on the Areopagus (Acts 17:28). However, even these few citations clearly indicate that the Stoic notion of God's fatherhood was basically an intellectual one, which could never be disjoined from the concepts of *"kosmos"* and *"logos"* in the Greek sense, that is, from the world as all-embracing and co-extensive with divinity and universal reason. Through his reasoning, man is capable of adapting himself to the divine order of the cosmos and to live according to universal nature. By doing so he is a "child of God." But the whole point is that here we find no concrete, personal relationship, involving in some way a love of predilection.

The true preparation for the Christian concept of God's fatherhood is to be found in the Old Testament and in Judaism. A few pointed texts will exemplify this tradition. Because of the covenant which God made with Israel, the people are His son. "Thus says the Lord: Israel is My son, My first-born" (Exod. 4:22). "You are children of the Lord, your God" (Deut. 14:1; cf. also Osee 11:1).[6] When in distress the people call to God: "For Thou art our Father, and Abraham has not known us, and Israel has been ignorant of us: Thou, O Lord, art our Father, our Redeemer, from everlasting is Thy name" (Isa. 63:16). "And now, O Lord, Thou art our Father, and we are clay: and Thou art our Maker, and we all are the works of Thy hands" (Isa. 64:7). And the Lord promises His eternal fidelity: "Can a woman forget her infant, so as not to have pity on the son of her womb? and if she should forget, yet will not *I* forget thee" (Isa. 49:15). Concerning the day of salvation, the prophet exclaims: "It shall be said to them: Ye are sons of the living God" (Osee 1:10). These ideas live on in later Judaism. Thus, Rabbi Aquiba used to say: "The Israelites are

---

[5] Poblenz (*Die Stoa*, I, 1948, pp. 69 and 108) thinks it possible that the Semitic origin of some of the older Stoics influenced their mode of representing God.

[6] Whenever possible, the citations of the Old Testament are taken from the Confraternity version; otherwise from the Douay-Rheims. (Trans.)

beloved, because they are called the sons of God. As a token of special love it is made known to them that they are called sons of God" (*Aboth*, 3, 14).

From these passages there appears a basic difference from the Stoa. Not all men can become children of God by their "reasoning"; only Israel or the Israelites are called such. And they are not called such because they have merited it by one or other intellectual or moral achievement, but because God has chosen them as His people. Only God's free choice constitutes the foundation of this filiation. It is based solely on His love and preference. The God of Israel is not void of affections; He is not an unfeeling, impersonal first cause of all things.[7] His love is neither abstract nor platonic; it is operative; it is an act of loving-kindness whereby God intervenes in the history of men, above all by electing His people, on whom He intends to found His new community. "Israel is My first-born."

It can however be ascertained that this name of Father is used for God in the Old Testament in a very provisional way, and especially that the whole relationship of God with His people was rather precarious because the behavior of Israel as a rule did not answer to its calling and election. Whenever "His people" is in trouble it calls to God as Father; then its sense of God's fidelity comes strongly to the fore. But on the whole its sonship is achieved only very imperfectly, and the prophecy's words refer in promise to a future of well-being. It is remarkable that II Cor. 6:18

[7] In the Bible, especially in the Old Testament, all kinds of human passions are attributed to God, such as anger, disgust, compassion. Under the influence of Greek philosophy, Christian theology teaches that one may not ascribe to God any emotions in the strict sense of the term, and calls these biblical expressions "anthropomorphisms," i.e., descriptions of God as though He were a man. This mannerism naturally has distinct advantages and in any case could not be avoided. But it could also entail great loss if it were to bring about a substitution of the abstract supreme being of reasoning for the living God of revelation. In its own naïve manner the Bible speaks about God much more realistically than does philosophy, because it contains God's own discourse on Himself and His activity, and not merely the abstractions of labored human reasoning.

places on the lips of the God of the Old Testament these words: "And I will welcome you in, and will be a Father to you, and you shall be My sons and daughters," though they are literally to be found nowhere in the Old Testament. The fatherhood of God is based on the act of His merciful election of Israel, but it becomes complete reality only through Jesus in the New Testament. The Old Testament points beyond itself to a time when the promises will be fulfilled.

The essential characteristic of the New Testament is, therefore, not that God is here given the name "Father" nor that individual people are called "children of God," [8] but that "Father" has become the ordinary and, as it were, obvious name for God; thus indicating that the truth to which the Old Testament pointed *is now achieved,* and that the name and the reality itself have been given us *by and in Jesus.* The promise has been fulfilled, the people of God, i.e., Israel, has been established, and Jesus is the mediator of this new and authentic relationship to God. Through union with Christ, we become children of God and God is our Father. Here the personal relationship is really in the foreground. It must not be overlooked that in the Gospel Jesus calls God His Father and Himself the Son in an entirely unique manner: "No one knows the Son except the Father; nor does anyone know the Father except the Son and him to whom the Son *chooses* to reveal Him" (Matt. 11:27). The divine sonship has become for us a visible and tangible reality in the mystery of the incarnation of the Son.

In the Synoptic Gospels Jesus does not speak about this truth with general terms or abstract suggestions; on the contrary, His words are extremely simple, concrete and vivid: "Be children of your Father in heaven" (Matt. 5:45: Become what you are, through a love for all!). "Are not two sparrows sold for a farthing? And yet not one of them will fall to the ground without your Father's leave. But as for you, the very hairs of your head are all numbered. Therefore do not be afraid" (Matt. 10:29, 30). Nowhere is the Gospel picture of God sketched more radiantly than in the parable

[8] This was already done in the Book of Wisdom, 2:13, 18.

of the prodigal son, which could more correctly be called the parable of the merciful father (Luke 15: 11–32). It is only to illustrate the father's response that the behavior of the two sons is described in detail. The primary intent of the parable is to teach us *God's* posture: as a perpetually solicitous and ever-forgiving father, such as can hardly be imagined in our ordinary human condition, uniting a spontaneous will to forgive with an enduring goodness toward the self-sufficient elder son. God is a good father to the dull, but righteous son, too. But He is never more so than when He forgives our sins—than when we make it possible for Him to forgive our sins.

We are almost too familiar with the story. Yet it is good to recall a few details, now that we are aware the parable draws a picture of God's demeanor and does not moralize or attempt to prescribe a rule of conduct for men. We too, much like the elder son, are inclined to find the description of the divine compassion exaggerated: "But while he was yet a long way off, his father saw him and was moved with compassion, and ran and fell upon his neck and kissed him." He allows him no time to utter his previously rehearsed petition: "Father, I have sinned against heaven and before thee. I am no longer worthy to be called thy son. . . ." He gets no further; his father simply will not allow him to finish and say: "Make me as one of thy hired men" (v. 19).

But the most beautiful part of the entire parable is in what has *not* been written. The pardon is so self-evident that it is not even reduced to words. The father simply does not respond to the halting confession of the son. He simply will not speak about it. "But the father said to the servants. Fetch quickly the best robe . . . and the ring . . . and sandals . . . and make merry." When among us, human beings, the wayward son or the disgraced daughter return to their parental home, such a reaction is hardly possible. Even the best parents who take in their child with love are not in a mood to celebrate; instead they feel somewhat ashamed and avoid publicity; and their friends will let the unpleasant affair pass unnoticed. But the father of the parable (who is no less than God!) gives no thought for the hush-hush of secrecy, nor even for the cloak of love, but calls for the gala costume. There is nothing to hide. There must be joy and music and festivity. And there is nothing to hush up. The child is not relegated to the rear room, he is honored publicly; deck him out with the fine robe and put a ring on his finger. Because my son "was dead and has come to life again; he was lost, and is found."

One may long reflect on this parable. There is no mention of a mother. God is alone, unrivaled in authority and power. One might surmise that the younger son wanted to go away, felt that he *must* go away, and, to give vent to his feelings, rebelled against the paternal authority and the proper respectability of his brother by ignoring all the values which had obtained in the family. It would be rather easy to reflect on him in terms of modern psychology; but not so on the father. He answers in no wise to the Freudian outline. The youngest son is the typical "lost son," but the father is not the typical father of the prodigal son, as he usually is found among us. He permits his growing child full liberty, even though there are risks attached to it. He gives the lad all that is his and lets him go his way. When things go wrong, the father is not disgraced. He does not reject him or disown him. He continues to recognize him as his own child no less than the other. This father, who is without sin, does not deny his own image. In contrast, earthly fathers often act as though the sins of their children were offenses not against God but against their own dignity, and as though the evil which their children commit was not within their own possibility. If in the parable no reference whatever is made to the past, this is done not because of shame, but because of unsurpassing love, which has pardoned both the sin and revolt so completely that nothing more remains to be said. Even the Old Testament perceived this authentic characteristic of God: "He will turn again, and have mercy on us: He will put away our iniquities: and He will cast all our sins into the bottom of the sea" (Mich. 7:19). "Thou has delivered my soul that it should not perish, Thou hast cast my sins behind Thy back" (Isa. 38:17).

TWO

The Coming of the Kingdom

"IN THIS MANNER therefore shall you pray: Our Father who art in heaven, hallowed be Thy name. Thy kingdom come . . ." (Matt. 6:9, 10). In what does this *hallowing of the name* consist? Above all in this, that God be acknowledged by men as the Lord and Father, that the transcendent and immanent concept of God which was outlined in the previous chapter persist, that men think of God as their Father who is in heaven, who is near us and yet infinitely surpasses us, that men be filled with respect for God and confidence in God. But the true hallowing of His name is accomplished only when He Himself ratifies His rule: Thy kingdom come. God's name is hallowed above all when He organizes His "kingdom" and establishes it "on earth as it is in heaven."

One might be inclined to view the Gospel picture of divinity, such as it was outlined above, as something static, as the simple acknowledgement of an idea, of a truth that has been revealed to us. All this is correct as far as it goes, but petitioning that His kingdom come, protects us from the danger of one-sidedness. It makes us realize that the reality of God such as it has been made known to us by the Master in the Gospels is not static but dynamic, that it is not a reality which is quiescent and self-contained but one which is active and operative.

In the three oldest Gospels, and hence also in the preaching of Jesus, the *kingdom of God* is the dominating idea, the expression of the dominant reality. When, in the beginning of his Gospel, Mark begins to narrate Jesus' public life, he writes: "And after John had been delivered up, Jesus came into Galilee, preaching the gospel of the kingdom of God" (1:14). Thus the Lord preached the kingdom of God primarily, and Himself only indirectly, so far as He had relationship to that kingdom, only gradually unveiling the central position which He occupied in it. The leading theme, and in a certain sense the only topic of His preaching is the kingdom of God. For Him there was no other basic value. Compared with it, everything else held second rank. And He was most desirous that His disciples should be animated with a similar outlook: "Seek first the kingdom of God and His justice, and all these things shall be given you besides" (Matt. 6:33). A precise insight into what the Master had in mind by this preaching is therefore of utmost importance, not only for biblical theology in the strict sense but also for what one may call the spirituality of the Gospels, because it is among the elements which define man's proper attitude toward God and divine revelation.

To begin with the expression itself, Matthew almost always uses the formula, "the kingdom of heaven"; whereas Mark and Luke always speak of the "kingdom of God"; and all three speak about "the kingdom of the Father" or simply of "the kingdom." It is generally agreed that there is no essential difference between the two formulas, since later Judaism tended to avoid the word "God" and used the term "heaven" or "heavens" as a customary substitute for the name of the godhead. This destroys a recurrent misunderstanding which consciously or unconsciously identifies the kingdom of heaven with heaven itself. In the Hebrew the expression is *malkut Yahweh* (*Elohim*); in Greek, *basileia tou theou,* which is ordinarily translated as "the kingdom of God." In our modern languages there is the difficulty that the term generally denotes a determined area of space, a territory over which someone rules as king, though occasionally it has other significations. But in the scriptural languages, Hebrew, Aramaic, and Greek, the meaning of the formula is much richer since its primary signification is not one of place or territory, but rather royal dignity or authority, especially the royal rule, the actual rule of a king.[1] The spatial or territorial nuance dominates in expressions such as "to enter into the kingdom of heaven," but is generally not in the center of focus. "Thy kingdom come" means rather: may Your rule be definitively established. "To receive the kingdom of God as a child" is to say the same as to accept God's authority as a child.

When we now begin to establish the exact meaning of these words, we must to a certain extent begin with a clean slate, with a temporary suspension of our already extant ideas concerning the kingdom of God, which naturally are not entirely incorrect, but neither are they, for that matter, completely exact. To mention just one thing, the kingdom of God in the Gospels is not simply heaven, nor is it to be automatically identified with the Church.

The kingdom is mentioned very often in the Gospels but it is never defined nor even described in any detail, since Jesus begins with a concept that was well known among His hearers. He corrects it and gives it a new depth of meaning, but again in an indirect manner through the various proclamations He makes *about* the kingdom of God. The difficulty is enhanced by the many and often apparently contradictory statements that are made concerning the kingdom so that we may rightly ask ourselves: Is it dominion or domain? Is it on earth or in heaven? In the hearts of men or something outside them? Does it exist in the present or is it still to come? In what follows, a few aspects of this rich notion, or better, of this great and unique reality will be examined so that conclusions may be readily drawn for a biblical spirituality.

No matter how obvious it may seem, it is of utmost importance to insist: the kingdom is the kingdom *of God*. Furthermore, this is the only qualification the evangelists give. It is God who rules over His kingdom and establishes His dominion, He alone. It is the marvel of God's own personal creative force. God alone

[1] In English this is properly the meaning of *kingship*. *Kingdom* in this sense is archaic. (Trans.)

makes it a reality, without any contribution on the part of man. Nowhere is this revealed more beautifully than in that brief, little known parable, which has been recorded only by Mark (4:26–29): "And He said: Thus is the kingdom of God, as though a man should cast seed into the earth, then sleep and rise, night and day, and the seed should sprout and grow without his knowing it. For of itself the earth bears the crop, first the blade, then the ear, then the full grain in the ear. But when the fruit is ripe, immediately he puts in the sickle because the harvest has come." With incredible mastery, since He uses nothing but the simple scene of a most ordinary occurrence of the countryside, the Lord suggests the basic truth of all revelation and even of redemption, which Western man keeps forgetting time and again. In a different place Jesus says to His disciples: "Do not be afraid, little flock, for it has pleased your Father to give you the kingdom" (Luke 12:32). They are to pray for the kingdom's coming, they are to proclaim it, but God alone effects it.

Although the establishment of the kingdom is entirely and exclusively God's work, this does not mean that men cannot exclude themselves from it or that they will automatically have part in it. On the contrary, extremely severe conditions are demanded of them. Precisely by preaching the kingdom, Jesus compels every individual to make a personal choice. (Here we have one of the wonderful elements in the Gospel, this respect for the personality, this respect for the liberty of man. Time and again Jesus appeals to the heart in the profound sense of the word; deliberately He places before man a decision which must be entirely his own, which must flow from his own unique and total responsibility. He comes to meet man, each man, with His invitation and waits for the answer. The answer, given freely, will either make a meeting possible or will be a denial and a departure. The Master has dared to permit man his liberty.) In order to partake in the kingdom it is not necessary to belong to a certain people or to a particular group, as was the opinion of many Jews at the time of Jesus. Neither external union with the Church nor even a charismatic union with Christ guarantees it: "Not everyone who says to Me, Lord, Lord, shall enter the kingdom of heaven; but he who does the will of My Father in heaven shall enter the kingdom of heaven. Many will say to Me in that day, Lord, Lord, did we not prophesy in Thy name, and cast out devils in Thy name, and work many miracles in Thy name? And then I will declare to them, I never knew you. Depart from Me, you workers of iniquity" (Matt. 7:21–23).

What then? What conditions does Jesus demand of the individual man, conditions which give such serious moral implications to His preaching? "The time is fulfilled, and the kingdom of God is at hand. Repent and believe in the Gospel" (Mark 1:15). Those are two basic demands: penance, or rather conversion, an inner turning about, an abandoning of former positions, a giving up of carefully accumulated assurances, of a false spiritual quiet and balance; and faith, the acceptance of the joyful news, confidence in Jesus, the conviction that in Him the kingdom of God is coming. The first points to the abandoning of the old, the second to the embracing of the new, but both belong together. And because the kingdom is solely God's work and always in the future, while we remain here on earth, these demands for conversion and acceptance remain in force, even for those who have long been Christians. In the beatitudes Jesus indicates in a different manner those who are fit for the kingdom of God: the poor, the meek, those who hunger and thirst and are persecuted (Matt. 5:3–10). And elsewhere: "Whoever does not accept the kingdom of God as a little child will not enter into it" (Mark 10:15). And in a paradoxical statement to the priests and ancients of the people, *honorable men:* "Amen I say to you, the publicans and harlots are entering the kingdom of God before you" (Matt. 21:31). This gives us some idea of how little value *our* standards are. In the demands placed by our Lord an inexorable earnestness comes to the fore. But at the same time it must be added that precisely because of this the kingdom of God is open to every man *as man*. Whatever distinguishes men and divides them—ancestry, talent, wealth or culture—carries no influence here. For the first time in the history of religion, salvation is proclaimed to all those, and to them alone, who are of good will. This message is meant for everyone. It knows no privileges.

It therefore also proclaims the perfect prize. After the remarkable praise for the Baptist, "Among those born of women there has not risen a greater," follows the unavoidable comparison: "Yet the least in the kingdom is greater than he" (Matt. 11:11). "Seek first the kingdom of God and His justice, and all these things shall be given you besides" (Matt. 6:33). The words, "and all these things," do not mean the superfluous things and luxuries of life, but the necessary clothing and daily bread, the things that we call the necessities of life; our Lord speaks here not to the wealthy, but to the simple people of Galilee. The kingdom of God is the hidden treasure and precious pearl of great price for which one joyfully sacrifices everything (Matt. 13:44–46), for which some even have "made themselves eunuchs" (Matt. 19:12).

Origen coined the word *autobasileia,* by which he wanted to indicate that Jesus is Himself the kingdom of God; the kingdom becomes visible in Him, first in the meanness and scandal of His earthly existence, and later, at His second coming, it will emerge with His glory. Seldom does Jesus speak expressly of the inner relationship existing between Him and the kingdom of God, first because His preaching was primarily directed at purifying the notion which the Jews already had of the kingdom and protecting it against an excessively nationalistic messianism which could easily attach itself to His person, as actually did happen in spite of all His efforts. But occasionally the inseparable bond between Himself and the kingdom is pointed out with a single word: "But if I cast out devils by the finger of God, then the kingdom of God has come upon you" (Luke 11:20). And later, when the conflict had become unavoidable, He proclaims without ambiguity that entrance into the kingdom depends on relationship to His person: "For he who would save his life will lose it; but he who loses his life for My sake and for the Gospel's sake will save it" (Mark 8:35). "For My sake and for the Gospel's sake." The connective is most meaningful, because the Gospel is nothing else than the proclamation of the kingdom of God. Similarly in Mark

10:29 we read about leaving home and family "for My sake and for the Gospel's sake," while in the parallel passage in Luke 18:29 it says simply: "for the sake of the kingdom of God." But if the kingdom of God and the Son of Man are so intimately connected in this economy, this means that the kingdom, even though it be the incomparably exalted divine miracle, now shares in the obscurity, in the humiliation and cross of Jesus. Its pure nature and its divine glory are now masked. The Church cannot see triumph in this eon.

In the last analysis it also means that in the person and preaching of Jesus the kingdom of God is already present and yet always coming. For our earthly eyes it is always in the future. We Christians are living for the *future;* we are Christians because of the future. To time's end we shall pray: Thy kingdom come. Only at the resurrection will it appear, permanent, public, glorious. It is the pre-eminent eschatological event. However, this term must be understood in light of the totality of the Christian doctrine of the last things. This Christian teaching also casts light on the mystery of the Church. That beautiful fulfillment which will be the completed kingdom of God is not exclusively future; it is already present in a cryptic manner, hidden as it were under a veil, just as during our Lord's earthly life His divine glory could be contemplated only by faith (John 1:14).

To say that the kingdom of God is coming refers therefore to God's activity in the history of men, His appearance among men through Jesus, His rule over men through the cross of Jesus —that is, through love, and at one time through His irresistible glory (Apoc. 1:7). It is the way, but not one that is laid at our feet or clear to our eyes, to the goal where God shall be "all in all" (I Cor. 15:28). Because it is essentially an eschatological, other-earthly quantum, it is not indentical with the Church. Even the Church, though filled with the powers of the kingdom by His Spirit, does not have sway over it. One might call the Church the organ of the kingdom of God.[2] *Ecclesia* (Church) and *basileia*

[2] See the superb treatise on the kingdom of God by Joseph Schmid, in *Das Evangelium nach Markus,* 2nd ed., Regensburg, 1950, pp. 25-30.

(kingdom) are closely related but not identical. The Church may not act as though the glorious and definitive kingdom of God had already appeared in her. Although it is not a purely human organization, having its origin in a free union of the faithful and thus "from below," and although it shares more than any other earthly society in the powers of the kingdom of God, the latter is nonetheless present in her only in a state of humiliation, in the darkness of faith and in the mystery of sacramental signs.

What this Gospel teaching can mean for the spiritual life is evident. It rescues us from the delusion that man by his own power and achievements can establish the kingdom of God on earth. It reveals the intrinsic deficiency of our standards, since the kingdom of God can in no way be estimated by human criteria. It admonishes us to be prudent, to understand that God does not need our work (regardless of His insistence that we work and preach, we always remain "unprofitable servants" [Luke 17:10]); it compels us to estimate the worth of our endeavors and organizations in a sound manner. It fills us with respect and esteem for the world of God, to which we are admitted only through grace. It frees us from the heresy of the self-sufficiency of activity and from every turbulent effort to reach that which is not ours to dispose of.

At the same time, however, Jesus' preaching on the ever-coming kingdom endows the genuinely Christian life with enormous dynamism. It renders utterly impossible any security of gain and all bourgeois opulence in the religious dimension. If we accept it through faith we will share in our own way in the free and enchanting movement and the strong current which quickened primitive Christianity. "And the spirit and the bride say, 'Come!' And let him who hears say, 'Come!' . . . Amen! Come, Lord Jesus!" (Apoc. 22:17, 20.) "May grace come! May this world pass away!" (*Didache,* 10, 6.) Strictly speaking, historical attitudes cannot be revived, and it is utterly impossible for us to arouse that same vehement longing for the immanent consummation which animated the first Christians. After so many centuries the Church has been firmly entrenched in our world, and we are more conscious of our Christian duty toward our fellow men. "World" no longer means for us, as it did for the Gnostics, the totality of irreparable evil, nor does it signify a phase to be overcome, as it does in the citation from the teaching (*Didache*) of the twelve apostles noted above. The word "world" is an appeal to our love for our fellow man, to our sense of apostolic responsibility. This more positive evaluation of the world as a task and a Christian possibility is a victory that has been gained over an all-too-destructive disdain. Yet this is true only on the condition that we know how to bear the burden of our "incarnation" in this earthly life without being burdened down by it, but with that liberty which is given us by that ancient Christian concept of the kingdom of God which has come and which will come without the effort of mankind.

THREE

The Ethic of the Sermon on the Mount

THE ETHIC OF THE KINGDOM of God is to be found in the aggregate of the three oldest Gospels, but above all in the many parables and in the Sermon on the Mount. The great theme of God's sovereignty gave a definite quality, an unmistakable overtone to all the exhortations of the Master, as they were apprehended by His hearers in all their purity and clarity. We, too, will be able to discern this, but only if we know how to transport ourselves in spirit into the situation of the disciples. There are parables which cannot possibly be understood except from the eschatological point of view. Jesus places His hearers at the great crisis: The kingdom of God is near, it is already present in His person! Convert! Believe! Now is the time of decision. One may not hesitate, even though it means giving up former outlooks and positions in order to attain to the kingdom of God. It is this situation of having to make a choice which cannot be put off that forms the point of some of the parables on the judgment. Whoever has the imagination and the courage to tackle an entirely new situation immediately, is fit for the kingdom of God. This, for example, is undoubtedly the meaning of the famous parable of the unjust steward, although this highly original little piece seldom gets the explanation it deserves (Luke 16:1–8a). And yet the moral is

35

clearly indicated in the text of the Gospel itself: "And the Master [1] commended the unjust steward, in that he had acted prudently" (16:8a). His cleverness consisted in his ability to discover immediately in the new situation, in which he suddenly found himself and which struck him like a catastrophe, the only way out that was left open to him and to follow it without scruple, fully aware of the end to which it was leading him. He was dismissed at once (v. 2). Verses 3 and 4 briefly indicate both the impasse and the suggested solution: "And the steward said within himself: What shall I do, seeing that my master is taking away the stewardship from me? To dig I am not able; to beg I am ashamed. I know what I shall do, that when I am removed from my stewardship they may receive me into their houses." Then follow quickly the devious measures he took without delay: "Take thy bond and sit down at once and write fifty, . . . write eighty. . . ." And the story is over, the "etching" is finished; again, the whole is reached with an extreme frugality of detail.

We are not told what finally happens to the steward, but everyone understands that his efforts were successful. Those who heard it could readily imagine such a tragic-comic situation in ancient Palestine, since there were rich landlords who frequently lived in foreign countries and thus simply could not do without trustworthy stewards. That is the whole story, and verse 8a gives the point. Jesus praises the cleverness of the man, and the parable is ended. Let the listeners apply the moral, let them fit the shoe to the correct foot.

If we place the parable in the framework of Jesus' preaching on the imminent and already present kingdom of God, all this becomes quite clear. Through our Lord's coming, through the word that He speaks, the situation of His hearers is suddenly and completely changed. They must behave like the steward who in

[1] The word has to be capitalized, since it refers to Jesus (e.g., 18:6) and not to the master of the steward, who has no reason whatever to praise the scoundrel. Furthermore, the point of the whole story is that the rich patron did *not* detect the deception; where else would the cleverness of the steward lie?

similar circumstances knew at once how to adapt himself and did not shrink from radical measures. Whoever clings to his old position, to his former manner of thinking, feeling, possessing, or even of existing, cannot follow Jesus. The parable has the same general direction as those other radical words preserved by Luke: "Let the dead bury their own dead," and: "No one, having put his hand to the plow and looking back, is fit for the kingdom of God" (9:60, 62). Jesus came to upset hearts and spirits in order to open them to the divine invasion which was occurring in our world through Him. God's sovereignty had truly arrived with Him, though its glorious manifestation was still to come. To this extent one can rightly speak with modern exegetes about an accomplished eschatology, about the final age that had been inaugurated through the incarnation and the revelation of the Lord.

It is not surprising that the "immoral" parable of the unjust steward was soon misunderstood, and one might even ask if Luke himself grasped its full significance. For what he adds immediately without any break—"For the children of this world are in relation to their own generation more prudent than are the children of light. And I say to you, make friends for yourselves with the mammon of wickedness"—is meant to be a mitigating and inoffensive re-interpretation, and has in any case led to the customary interpretation. But the admonition to acquire friends by means of one's *own* money and by almsgiving cannot have been the original conclusion of the parable.

Likewise the ethic (to continue with the expression) developed in the Sermon on the Mount (Matt. 5:7) has a similar slant. The beatitudes serving as introduction posit the completely unworldly conditions which must be fulfilled if the disciples are to share in the kingdom. And a passage such as Matt. 5:25, 26 ("Come to terms with thy opponent quickly while thou art with him on the way; lest thy opponent deliver thee to the judge, and the judge to the officer, and thou be cast into prison. Amen I say to thee, thou wilt not come out from it until thou has paid the last penny") must not be understood as an exhortation to purely human prudence or proper concern for one's well-being. It is a highly condensed parable, having in the background the coming judgment of God (for the coming of the kingdom is accompanied by the judgment and the decisive separation of the wheat from the weeds); this is what lends these few verses their character of urgent warning (see also Luke 12:57–59).

For some Protestants the Sermon on the Mount is only a mirror held up to us by Jesus to help us recognize our sins and to make us understand that we are not capable of fulfilling the commands of Jesus. "Whence do you know your misery? From the Sermon on the Mount." One might call this a Pauline interpretation (and a lop-sided one at that) of the Sermon on the Mount. For many Catholics, on the contrary, the Lord is exclusively the lawgiver, by which they often infer that the Sermon on the Mount is meant only for an elite, whereas they themselves are bound by the ten commandments of God and the commandments of the Church. Both suppositions are wrong.

Chapters 5 to 7 of Matthew's Gospel represent the Lord as the new and greater Moses, who with authority proclaims His teaching on the mountain. It is a grand outline of a program which goes back at least in part to an address that was really delivered by Jesus,[2] and is partly compiled by the evangelist and supplemented by various logia. The program which it discloses contains the outline of the new and "abundant justice" of the kingdom of God, which must characterize His disciples and is contrasted with the justice of the Scribes and Pharisees. The latter parallels in its basic lines the rabbinic justice of the Talmud. For the Jew, "justice" was the great cultic watchword, whose whole content might be described as the "ideal, pious life," or "holiness."

The introduction to the Sermon consists of eight beatitudes, which already contained the whole program in a nucleus and breathed a totally new spirit, and in the adjoining axioms about the salt of the earth and the light of the world.

[2] This is evident from the shorter parallel passage in Luke 6:20–49, which is occasionally called "The Sermon in the Open Air." This is composed of four beatitudes, four woes, the commandment of love for one's enemy, the proscription of judgment over others, and the exhortation to make thought and action agree.

In the first part Jesus opposes his teaching to the Old Law, which He does not repeal but "perfects" and "completes," i.e., He returns it to its roots and transcends it (5:17-48). This passage is remarkably set off and enclosed as a unit by the bewildering command: "You therefore are to be perfect, even as your heavenly Father is perfect" (5:48). After this the Lord contrasts His ideal with the pious practices of the Pharisees,—almsgiving, prayer and fasting,—by demanding inwardness and spirit above all (6:1-18).

In the second part Jesus speaks more positively and directly of the attitudes and activity which must characterize the new life, such as detachment, liberty, trust (6:19-7:23). This section contains the well known "Franciscan" passage (6:25-34).

The conclusion is composed of two axioms about hearing and doing (7:24-27). What the evangelist then adds about the astonishment of the multitude and about the purely spiritual but informal authority of Jesus is simply beautiful. Naturally, only a few aspects of this constitution of the Christian life and Christian spirituality can be considered here.

As far as the distinct "form" of the Sermon on the Mount is concerned, whoever considers it as a book of law in the technical sense, as a code, will never be able to grasp it. It does not consist exclusively of precepts, but, for example, also includes alluring invitations in the form of blessings or "beatitudes" (which nevertheless are disguised demands). Above all, one must realize that it does not formulate its precepts in the manner of a book of law. Everything is concrete, much of it sounds paradoxical, some of its sayings are even ironical. In reading the Gospels we must never forget that Jesus did not write a thing,[3] and that all His words were spoken, so that we must supplement by our imagination the sound of His voice, His general bearing, the look of His eyes, which all were surely quite different from the pulpit accent we have grown accustomed to associate with them. "If someone strike thee on the right cheek, turn to him the other also; and if anyone would go to law with thee and take thy tunic, let him take thy cloak as well" (5:39, 40). "When thou fast,

[3] Except once (to the shame of those for whom He wrote) in the sand (John 8:8).

anoint thy head" (6:17). "Therefore do not be anxious about
tomorrow; for tomorrow will have anxieties of its own" (6:34).
There simply is no thought that we can apply to such texts a strict
and literal interpretation which is proper for a book of law. One
must not understand the Sermon on the Mount *au pied de la
lettre,* but that does not mean that it lacks earnestness. The type
of men we are—with a Western temperament, modern outlook,
etc.,—can hardly imagine that binding precepts can be given in
the form of paradoxes. If we cannot take commands literally, we
are at a loss and simply do not know what to do with them. But
Jesus pronounces His most earnest injunctions with playful ease
in parables and imagery, and with most surprising turns of phrase.

In spirit, too, the Sermon on the Mount differs from a code of
law, which is always necessarily directed at the minimum, having,
as it were, its feet on the floor and not trying to reach the ceiling.
But Jesus constantly aims at the maximum, pointing to the heights,
to the ceiling,—and at that, a ceiling that has an open roof and
allows us to cast our eyes on the very heavens. To take just one
example among many, let us look for a moment at Matt. 5:21, 22:
"You have heard that it was said to the ancients: Thou shalt not
kill; and that whoever shall murder shall be liable to judgment.
But I say to you that everyone who is angry with his brother
shall be liable to judgment." The Old Law forbade murder; this
is the indispensable minimum.[4] Jesus subjects anger to the same
penalty. He extends the commandment, He expands the obligation. Even this does not tell the whole story. What He really does
is to make the prohibition absolute. He removes all restringent
determinations and, consequently, elevates the very character of
the precept, since any determination necessarily limits and restricts.
It is impossible, speaking in terms of daily life, that someone
should never "be angry with his brother." May one therefore say,
"I will just ignore this command because it is utterly impossible
to observe it anyway?" That would indeed be the correct attitude

---

[4] But this does not mean that Jewish law had no care for the interior aspect
of things. Jesus has in mind a concrete outlook, which had a specific historical reality but will always remain a general human possibility.

if it were a question merely of a "precept" in the legal sense of the word. But Jesus presents authoritatively the obligatory direction toward which our liberty, our disposition and readiness must be orientated.

Likewise in the first portion of the Sermon on the Mount, the "fulfillment" of the Old Law, which seems to be the most legalistic and to afford us some hold, the same bewildering radicalism is present as elsewhere. Every human being, including the Christian, is subject to judgment, falls under the verdict, and from this point of view the Protestant opinion mentioned at the beginning of this chapter is correct. Because of the legalistic and moralistic inclination of Catholics, the notion of being sinners and thus falling short of the mark tends to paralyze their moral impulse. But Jesus desires exactly the opposite. He wishes to deprive man of every religious and moral self-sufficiency and to summon him, thus liberated from the deepest root of egoism and being "poor in spirit," to fulfill the heavenly ethic of the child of God.

In the Sermon on the Mount, as the ethic of the kingdom which is always coming, there is an awe-inspiring dynamism which of necessity is missing in a lawbook. It simply removes our favorite distinction between what is compulsory and what is free, between those things which are of *obligation* or of *supererogation*. It does not allow man the feeling of having done enough or "something special." "Anyone who even looks with lust at a woman has already committed adultery with her in his heart." "I say to you not to swear at all." "Do not let thy left hand know what thy right hand is doing." "Do not judge, that you may not be judged." "All things whatever you would that men should do to you, even so do you also to them." There is no qualification and hence no termination. However, this also shows that the Sermon on the Mount never deprives man of his free initiative. On the contrary, in every situation it places him before the task of creative, Christian responsibility. It gives no directives, but points in a direction; it places us on a road that is endless but not without an objective: "You therefore are to be perfect, even as your heavenly Father is perfect."

In the Gospel our Lord places men before an ideal of life which without exaggeration may be said to be unattainable in this eon: for if it were to be accomplished completely and actually, then our planet would be transformed into the "new earth where justice dwells." But the Christian is obliged to strive after this ideal without ever being able to realize it fully in this life. This is the meaning of the beatitude: "Blessed are they who hunger and thirst for justice, for they shall be satisfied" (Matt. 5:6), once the kingdom of God has come in glory. For the time being the Christian is the one who is poor, who mourns, who longs ardently and is persecuted, never the one who possesses or is content. Nonetheless, this unattainable goal is intended for all who desire to follow the Lord. Christians are not free to reject this ideal as a superfluity or as an impossible luxury. One cannot apply the distinction between evangelical precepts and "counsels" to the Sermon on the Mount. It was not proclaimed for an elite but for all who wish to be disciples of the Lord, and that as an obligation, albeit as an obligation of a very special kind.

If now we turn our eyes from the evangelical to the ecclesiastical reality, we are immediately faced by the question of where the many laws which have come into being in the course of time and are being constantly implemented with new specifications, find their justification. There is a tremendous difference between the spirit of the Sermon on the Mount, for instance, and the official lawbook of the Church, which is indeed a real codex. A similar problem will face us later when we consider the Pauline concept of liberty and its adventures in Christendom. It is extremely difficult to treat briefly and to some degree satisfactorily this problem which is truly an annoying one for many Christians of our age.

In the first place one must point out certain unavoidable facets in its historical development. Every spiritual movement derives its origin from the intuition of some gifted individual, about whom a small group of disciples gather as intimate associates. These are so inspired by the word and example of their master that they almost acquire his unique pre-eminence; in them his vision acquires such purity of form as it will never again possess in a later period. It is the period in which the wide world has hardly become aware of the new birth in its womb, but which is not of its spirit. It is also the period before the idea has gained many followers and hence, before a certain adaptation to the level of the crowd with its ensuing rules and specifications has become necessary. One is reminded of Francis of Assisi with his first disciples, or the small group that surrounded Loyola on Montmartre. Because of increase in number, time and range, there will later be an unavoidable lessening in purity of intention and intensity. The first inspiration continues to exist in the growing community as a leaven which is constantly discovered anew and revitalized by charismatic and prophetic personages, who are capable of experiencing the original impulse as their own.

One may apply this to Christendom as a spiritual movement initiated by our Lord. The primitive communities lived in His spirit, and of their own accord gave material expression to the concept of Christian fraternity. However, one must add at once that the primitive Christian ideal was the more difficult to preserve in its purity and original spontaneity to the degree that it surpasses the capacity of the natural man. In the epistles to the Corinthians we sense the struggle of the Apostle to introduce the Christian ideal of life and to let it operate unhindered in a new milieu, which was totally Hellenistic. There we are accordingly introduced to "precepts" properly so called, such as those for the governing of their liturgical assemblies (I Cor. 11 and 14).

It is therefore incorrect to imagine that in the Bible there are no juridical elements. This is evident for the Old Testament with its many laws. The New Testament, too, contains regulations of a sort to determine definitely the behavior of the Christians, both as individuals and as a community. Christ Himself did not hesitate at times to speak His mind openly on juridical matters, and these words of the Master are rightly considered by the Church as normative for Christian life and as laws in the strict sense of the word. Read, for example, Mark 10:1–12 on the indissolubility of matrimony. Even before the time of St. Paul, all such pronouncements were beyond discussion. They were fixed norms, binding as well in Rome and in Corinth, as in Antioch (cf. I Cor. 7:10). The rudiments of government and legislation were of necessity connected with the foundation of the Church as a society which must exist in time and space until the Parousia, and are expressly credited to Christ by the evangelists (Matt. 16:17–19; 18:18; John 21:15–17, etc.). The same principle is operative in the Pauline pagan-Christian communities and, to judge from I Corinthians, even before the writing of the pastoral epistles.

It was unavoidable that this juridical element should become more prominent in proportion as the Church grew in number and spread over the world. As long as the whole was composed of several small units whose religion bore an entirely unearthly character and nourished itself with an ardent expectation of the consummation, this element remained in the background, although it was always present in nucleus. But the delay of the Parousia (see for example II Pet. 3) occasioned a more permanent foundation of the Church, even though the persecutions of the first centuries and the hostility of the Roman Empire rendered a proper establishment impossible for the time being. All this was changed with the acceptance of the Church by Constantine, which resulted in Christians being changed from the persecuted and outlawed to the acknowledged and even prominent citizens of an earthly empire, and at times even to persecutors of their former opponents. It is not necessary to continue here with the later history of the (Western) Church. It suffices to point out that the historical bond of this church with Rome and the inheritance of the Roman genius for governance were instrumental in the evolution of a more specifically juridical development.

In spite of these general considerations and all historical contingencies, many upright Christians still regard the considerable role played by the legal and juridical element in the Catholic Church as opposed to the spirit of the Gospel. For this reason the most important thing that can be affirmed here is the following: *We ourselves* are unfaithful to the spirit of the Gospel, *we* remain constantly under the maximum which our Lord, in the Sermon on the Mount, proposes as the Christian normal. It is our own fault, and our Christian inadequacy makes the multiplicity of laws unavoidable and gives the potentialities for legal development which were latent in the historical situation of the Western Church a powerful impetus, and even a certain hypertrophy. That a truly universal Church, as is the Catholic Church, should be able to exist, at least in this eon, without a closely knit organization and without a far-reaching administrative and juridical apparatus is sheer illusion. It is always possible to discuss the problem of the necessary and unavoidable amount of this element in certain determined circumstances. But it is also certain that, in principle, it decreases as Christian holiness increases. To the degree that we Catholics verify the Sermon on the Mount in our personal lives, we transcend the juridical and render it superflous. Our sins make it necessary—*not* our sins in the Gospel sense of the acknowledged sinfulness of all men, but the fact that we selfishly refuse to accept the Gospel vision which does not ask what is obligatory but asks what is possible and conformable to the perfection of the heavenly Father.

If the term were not in danger of falling into discredit, one might call the Sermon on the Mount a preliminary draft of Christian situation ethics. Starting from the fundamental situation of the Christian, it outlines the religious and moral behavior which must always characterize him as such. His actions flow from his being; and this basic nature, this inherent situation of the Christian, is thus described by Jesus: The disciple is a child of the heavenly Father, he is a member of the kingdom of God, he has fellowship with brothers and sisters, he lives in the world of matter and of men who can fail to appreciate him and persecute him. Next, there is the host of concrete, changing situations, innumerable and unforeseeable, in which it is the duty of the Christian to work out his fundamental situation by creatively giving to each concrete situation a Christian meaning, by responding to it as a child of God and a sharer in the kingdom. In the Sermon on the Mount our Lord repeatedly gives shape to His "ideal" through the help of such individual situations; see, for example, 5: 39–42; 6:17. Such words do not contain commands in our sense of the term, but rather examples, models. When Jesus was Himself struck on the cheek, He protested (John 18:22, 23). Even though this admits uncontestable principles such as the prohibition of adultery, it is still not determined in every aspect; by its very nature it is opposed to all legalistic and casuistic manipulation. This may be necessitated by the sins of Christians; nevertheless it does indicate a drop below the standard of the Gospel.

It seems worthy of note that the complete and unattainable ideal of the Sermon on the Mount does not oppress or depress weak, sinful man, but on the contrary lifts him up and gives him comfort. Its mysterious attractiveness can above all be attributed to its candor, to the invigorating expanse of its spiritual terrain. Nothing is intolerant or narrow-minded; the true dimensions of our existence are laid bare. Jesus makes an appeal to man's creative liberty and no matter how exalted His demands may be, they bear the marks not of chains which enslave but of possibilities which liberate. They have this character, however, only because of the person standing back of these words, in whom they have become reality and have appeared to us as human possibility. This is the foremost reason why these few pages of the New Testament keep attracting men. They are the true description of a human life that has actually been lived. They have become incarnate in the New Man, the last Adam, who by His life, death, and resurrection has become for each of us the only authentic human possibility. They shall always remain the *Magna Carta* of Christian spirituality.

FOUR

The Two Commandments

THOUGH THE ENGLISH POET, Dylan Thomas, died while still a young man, he was able to pen the following introduction to the collection of his poems: "These poems, with all their crudities, doubts and confusions, are written for the love of Man and in praise of God and I'd be a damn fool if they weren't." The Alexandrian Jew, Philo, contemporary of Jesus and Paul, expresses the same thought in his own, rather verbose and impersonal way: "Among the multitudinous individual truths and doctrines which are considered here, two principles are outstanding: the one concerns relationship toward God through piety and holiness, and the other deals with the relationship toward fellow man through fraternal charity and justice" (*De spec. leg.,* II, 63). The modernity of the poet consists in his placing love for man first and capitalizing Man, as is proper in our anthropocentric age. Perhaps one ought better say that it is this which betrays his Christian character. For the command of love of neighbor is the Christian command *par excellence.*

In the Gospel we read: "But the Pharisees, hearing that He had silenced the Sadducees, gathered together. And one of them, a doctor of the law, putting Him to the test, asked Him, 'Master, which is the great commandment in the Law?' Jesus said to him: 'Thou shalt love the Lord thy God with thy whole heart, and with thy whole soul, and with thy whole mind.' This is the greatest and the first commandment. And the second is like it, 'Thou shalt love thy neighbor as thyself.' On these two commandments depend the whole Law and the Prophets" (Matt. 22:34-40; and also Mark 12:28-31; Luke 10:25-28).

It may possibly come as a surprise to the Christian reader that both commandments are borrowed from the Old Testament and even formulated according to the old style. The commandment about the love of God is found in Deuteronomy (6:5) and that of love of neighbor in Leviticus (19:18). In what then does the Christian newness consist? Certainly not in an annulment of the old commandments, since the Decalogue is explicitly affirmed by Jesus (see Matt. 19:18, 19). It consists primarily in this, that Jesus, in opposition to Pharisaism (*all* Pharisaism, regardless of form or age), accented the centralizing unity of the divine will. According to the doctrine of the Synagogue there were in the Torah, the Old Law, 613 instructions of which 365 were precepts and 248 prohibitions. Furthermore, to all this there was added an extremely complicated interpretation. The Jew of Jesus' time found himself face to face with an endless multiplicity of commandments which obstructed his view of "the good and acceptable and perfect will of God" (Rom. 12:2). This religious perplexity prompts the striking question of the rich young man: "Which commandments?" and the query about "the greatest commandment" (Mark 12:28; Matt. 22:36). The learned literally lost themselves in endless discussions over the importance of particular prescriptions, while the unlearned lacked a focal point from which light could be cast on the whole complex. In opposition to all this confusing multiplicity, Jesus places a saving oneness.

Unity, and not duality. Love of God and love of man are not two independent principles. They cannot be separated in Christendom. It is difficult even to distinguish them. Here we find the basic originality of Jesus; i.e., the place of honor which love of neighbor holds in His doctrine. It is the second commandment, but *like to the first*. This is the great restoration. Henceforth religion is unthinkable without love of man. Every religion based on faith in a personal God places piety in the first rank. But

Christian piety expresses itself and finds its fulfillment in love for man. "I desire mercy, and not sacrifice"; the cry of the Old Testament prophet (Osee 6:6) is twice placed by Matthew on the lips of Jesus (9:13; 12:7; cf. 23:23). What this means in the concrete is explained by the Master in the Sermon on the Mount: "If thou art offering thy gift at the altar, and there rememberest that thy brother has anything against thee, leave thy gift before the altar and go first to be reconciled to thy brother, and then come offer thy gift" (Matt. 5:23, 24). In his preaching, Jesus does not enter into further discussion of the Old Testament precept of love for God. He simply ratifies it. It is the primary precept. But what is new is that He constantly proclaims and explains the commandment of love for neighbor. John repeats the thought of the Master in its purest form when in His farewell address he has Him declare: "This is *My* commandment, that you love one another" (15:12).

In Judaism the precept of fraternal charity was by no means disregarded; on the contrary, it occupied an honorable place. Judaism was already aware of the golden rule, at least in its negative form: "Do not do unto others what you would not have done to yourself. This is the whole Law. All the rest is interpretation." In the *Didache* (I, 2) we read: "The world is founded on three things: on the Law, on religion, and on works of charity." Philo dedicates a detailed chapter to "philanthropy," love of man (*De Virt.,* 51 ff.). And these references could be multiplied many times over.[1] However, even when abstracting from the restriction of the concept "neighbor," which we will treat shortly, one must conclude that in Jewish theology and morals not charity but justice was the dominating factor. That Jesus gave love and not justice the central position is considered even by orthodox Jews of our day as an essential variation from authentic Jewish doctrine.[2]

---

[1] For examples, see E. Stauffer, in *Theologisches Woerterbuch zum N.T.,* I, pp. 41–44.

[2] See J. Klausner: *Jesus von Nazareth,* 3rd ed., Jerusalem, 1952, pp. 527 f. Concerning Paul, the same author writes: "Paul spoke of Christian charity, which is really nothing else than Jewish love in mystical coloring, until

That Jesus did recognize the value of justice as the basis for social life is evident from various sayings having an unmistakable ring of authenticity about them, which the evangelists have preserved for us: "Render, therefore, to Caesar the things that are Caesar's, and to God the things that are God's" (Matt. 22:21). He defends the unassailable rights of family and marriage against the clever distinctions which were invoked in favor of priestly and male egoism (Matt. 15:1–9; 19:1–12). One might go so far as to say that His golden rule ("All things whatever you would that men should do to you, even so do you also to them" [Matt. 7:12]) includes the practice of justice as a necessary element, since everyone desires above all that right be done him and that he receive what is due him. Christian charity does not annul justice; it completes it by exceeding it and by giving the neighbor more than his due. In this it reflects the mercy of the heavenly Father, who finds delight in the unmerited remitting of sins; the conduct of our Lord, who preferred to associate with sinners more than with the just, and stated that He came for the sake of the "sick" and not for the "healthy" (Luke 15:1–2; Mark 2:17 ff.). As a willingness to forgive, it is based on the realization that no man can claim any rights before God, and that we (all of us who are "evil") can rely only on His grace. Time and again it is precisely this point that shows the indissoluble bond between religion and ethic and the complete identification of our relation to God with that to our fellow men. "Forgive us our debts as we *have already forgiven* our debtors" (according to the original text [Matt. 6:12; cf. vv. 14–15]). "Do not judge and you shall not be judged; do not condemn and you shall not be condemned. Forgive, and you shall be forgiven; give, and it shall be given to you; good measure, pressed down, shaken together, running over, shall they pour into your lap. For with what measure you measure, it shall be measured to you." (As is often the case in the New Testament, all these passive forms are a discreet way of indicating God's manner of

---

he forgot to accentuate *justice*, without which love is indeed a firm basis for individual life, but not for a social and a national existence" (*Von Jesus zu Paulus,* Jerusalem, 1950, pp. 516 f.).

acting. There is therefore no question here of human retribution in the sense of, "When you bounce a ball, you must look for a rebound" [Luke 6:37-38; cf. also Matt. 18:23-35]).

Nonetheless, it remains undeniably true that Jesus placed the Old Testament dictum, "Love your neighbor as yourself," right in the middle of His own doctrine, giving it an entirely new meaning and completely different dimensions from what it had formerly. We must subject this touchstone of the Gospel to a brief analysis.

The precept of fraternal charity presupposes in the first place that the Christian love himself (*"as yourself"*). Jesus does not dwell on this point since this love of self can normally be taken for granted. Even modern-day preachers seldom emphasize the theme, although one may doubt whether this is right, since *true* love of self is not as common in our social life as is commonly imagined. It must be properly distinguished from a wrong type of self-love, which is selfishness or egoism, the fatal and universal consequence of original sin. This distinction is extremely important, since the war against selfishness must not degenerate into aggressiveness against one's self or even into unconscious aversion for one's self. When Jesus says, "Love thy neighbor as thyself," He implicitly demands self-love. St. Thomas, too, teaches that one can and even ought love one's self with a supernatural love (IIa IIae, qq. 25 and 26). In actual fact, however, real love of self, which is the basis for love of neighbor and love of God, is quite often prominently missing. It presupposes a certain spiritual maturity, of which it is the external expression. It is quite probable that in our present (Western) civilization, with its multiple standards, this maturity is reached with greater difficulty and at a later period in life than in earlier periods of time. Let it be noted in passing that this fact bears serious consequences for the rearing and especially for the religious and moral formation of the young.

It would naturally be incorrect to suppose that religious formation can begin only after the natural development has been completed, because the religious interest is an essential component of human nature. There must therefore be a simultaneous development, a related evolution of the human and the religious experience, but always in such wise that the human formation is just one step ahead of the religious development.[3] The biological and psychological foundation for a more or less premeditated formation must always be present. The great danger consists in what I would like to call "anticipation." Attempts are frequently made to introduce adult religion among people who are not adults, to erect a full-blown moral edifice on an insufficient human foundation. People who are not yet spiritually mature are urged on to the perfection of the Christian life; and moral maturity is too readily computed according to the years of a person's age. The authentic exemplification of Christendom ought to be considered as the florescence of human existence, as the full bloom of nature and grace combined. Once again, this does not mean that the religious formation must wait till the child has grown up; but it does mean that one must administer it prudently, that one choose to rely on the casual pedagogic situation, and preserve some confidence in the nature of man.

The implicit command for self-love is enjoined because we cannot really love our neighbor if we do not love ourselves. In what does this love of self consist? In the first place (and possibly also in the last) in this, that we have squarely met our own selves and have come to know and appreciate ourselves. One must use here such an expression as "to meet oneself squarely," since no one begins with a clean slate. The fruit of the tree of knowledge is both sweet and bitter and an increase of self-knowledge opens a vista into an abyss which a child cannot see. To love myself means to learn how to limit and ground myself; to accept myself lovingly as a creature, and even as an image of God in my own limited but inimitable reality. It also means the accepting of my darker sides, my shadows, even the possibility of the evil which I did not do, but might have done as well as any other man, and in which I somehow have a mysterious share because of our common nature.

[3] Development is to be taken here especially in the sense of purposive formation, such as is generally stressed strongly in our concrete religious educational program; generally speaking, the indirect system really merits preference.

Since we are all "evil," to use Jesus' expression, evil—every human evil—is my real personal possibility even though it may not now be an actuality. The point is that I recognize that no evil whatever which is done by man is entirely strange to me, but constitutes a real and not merely a theoretical possiblity within me. Not to acknowledge this is, in the last instance, only because of a deceptive pride or repression, because of which I unconsciously refuse to behold and acknowledge myself in all my potentialities. The last condition will occur more commonly than the former.

And yet, for the exercise of fraternal charity it is necessary to understand with the ancient poet that nothing human is foreign to me. Again, this is not meant in the sense that true self-love precedes fraternal charity in the order of time. It is precisely through love of my neighbor that I discover myself and build up my own personality. A fruitful cooperation of love of self and love of neighbor is indispensable, otherwise I cannot possibly love my neighbor "as myself"; otherwise I will regard him as a stranger, as one who does not concern me.[4] Otherwise the possibility of hatred has been already established. "If you were of the world, the world would love what is its own. But because you are not of the world, but I have chosen you out of the world, therefore the world hates you" (John 15:19). Aversion and aggressiveness will frequently arise simply because I do not know or acknowledge one of the possibilities of my own personality. A person wants to eliminate or even destroy that "strangeness" which he projects into others. One hates those whom one knowingly considers as strange, as not being one's self, whereas in reality they represent one of our possibilities, and exactly the one we are trying to hide with shame. This throws light on many of the unbelievable doings of the War (and even later) and on the ruinous influence of modern propaganda, which necessarily works with black-white contrasts and feels a need for having or creating scapegoats, so as to foster an aggressiveness which is spawned from fear and aversion. But Christ freely chose to become a scapegoat for us all.

[4] There seems to be an old Chinese proverb to the effect that: "To forgive another the fact that he is different is the beginning of wisdom."

"Jesus, that He might sanctify the people by His blood, suffered outside the gate. Let us therefore go forth to Him outside the camp, bearing His reproach" (Heb. 13:12–13). "For our sakes He made Him to be sin who knew nothing of sin" (II Cor. 5:21). Paul urges Christians to bear one another's burdens (Gal. 6:2). What burden is heavier than the sinful and hateful element that exists also within ourselves?

Christ thereupon gave a new meaning to the notion of "neighbor," by removing all limitations. In the Old Testament, as also in contemporary Judaism, the concept was practically limited by kinship in race and local proximity; that is to say, by a sort of concentricity which measures all things from myself as the central point.[5] My neighbors are those who are nearest me, my family, neighbor, tribe, fellow tradesmen, race. And thus it becomes a static, predetermined concept, depending on accidental situations. Jesus deprived the existing notion of neighbor of its original meaning and freed it from all these particularizations. He transferred the central point from man to God and proclaimed the love of one's enemy as the hallmark *par excellence* of His disciples: "You have heard that it was said, 'Thou shalt love thy neighbor, and shalt hate thy enemy.' But I say to you, love your enemies, do good to those who hate you, and pray for those who persecute and calumniate you, so that you may be children of your Father in heaven, who makes His sun to rise on the good and the evil, and sends rain on the just and the unjust. You therefore are to be perfect even as your heavenly Father is perfect" (Matt. 5:43–48). One may also affirm that He Himself, the new Man, has been set by God as the central point of our circle: "Amen I say to you, as long as you did it for one of these, the least of My brethren, you did it for Me" (Matt. 25:40). For the Christian, therefore, every man is his neighbor.

But this universality must be understood in a concrete manner; it cannot be taken abstractly as meaning humanity in general. Christian love of neighbor is not some humanitarian sentiment

[5] For details (to which belong the possibility of hatred as well as the first spark of love for one's enemy) see Ps. 108; Prov. 25:21.

about humanity based in Stoic fashion on the sharing of a common nature or of universal reason. It is always personal, even individual, and directed toward whoever happens to be "near." Somewhere in the novel, *The Brothers Karamazov,* Dostoyevsky distinguishes between the distant neighbor and the close neighbor. Jesus is concerned with the latter. Everyone can be my neighbor, can become my neighbor in a certain situation; but not all men are so actually. Even the pious man of the Old Testament comprehended this when he wrote: "Man may be merciful to his fellow man, but the Lord's mercy reaches all flesh" (Sir. 18:11). Only God can truly love all men.

What then did Jesus really do with the concept "neighbor?" He made of it a notion that is of itself unlimited and unconditioned, defined only by the concrete situation in which one finds himself. My neighbor is the person with whom I find myself in a circumstance of proximity, that is, anyone with whom I by my love establish a relation of nearness, which in turn engenders a response. It is not determined beforehand who is my neighbor; anyone can become this. It is he, toward whom *in concreto* I have a relation of neighborliness, not the one whom I may casually meet, but him with whom I hold communication. My neighbor is the one, anyone at all, whoever he may be, whom I wish to encounter in the total concrete situation of my being-in-the-world and not because of something which has been added to my human status.

Our Lord teaches us this in an inimitable manner in the parable on the Good Samaritan (Luke 10:25-37), a concrete illustration which is far more telling than all general considerations, and gave the answer to the theoretic question of the lawyer: Who is my neighbor? This question was occasioned by the reference to the two commandments. The response shows anew that the originality of Jesus' preaching consisted especially in His doctrine on love of neighbor. This in turn immediately casts new light on the precept of love of God. Besides the robbed and wounded traveler, there in his passive role, three other personages appear in the parable. They are a priest, a levite, and a Samaritan, of whom the first two were much "closer" to the victim, not only in the Jewish view, but also in that of mankind generally. The Samaritan belonged to the semi-strange, and therefore estranged, people. All three chance on a fortuitous situation (v. 31) in which they bear a special relationship to the unfortunate traveler. Of all three the Master says explicitly that they "saw" him. However, for the priest and levite, both of whom are kinsmen and even belong to the officially pious class, their acquaintance remains a chance meeting. Only with the stranger does it become communication.

It is noteworthy how the text of the Gospel describes with succinct sobriety various phases in Christian charity: awareness, sympathy, a simple but expressive deed. "But a certain Samaritan, as he journeyed, came upon him, and seeing him, was moved with compassion. And he went up to him and bound up his wounds, pouring on oil and wine. And setting him on his own beast, he brought him to an inn and took care of him. And the next day he took out two denarii and gave them to the innkeeper and said, 'Take care of him; and whatever more thou spendest, I, on my way back, will repay thee.'" Christian love of neighbor is preeminently practical. The point of the parable may startle us: "Which of these three," Jesus asked the lawyer, "in thy opinion proved himself neighbor to him who fell among the robbers?" And the man naturally answered: "He who took pity on him." And Jesus said to him, "Go and do thou also in like manner." Here we see how dynamic and concrete the notion of neighbor is for Jesus. We may ask: Were not then the priest and the levite neighbors to the traveler? Jesus denies it, because they did not behave like neighbors, like people who wished to be near and let themselves become personally entangled in the situation of another which would somehow or other infringe on their independence. One is truly a neighbor only through love and mercy, through a deliberate availability. In that sense "neighbor" becomes synonymous with Christian.

Love, placed as it is by our Lord as the supreme "law" of the Christian life, does not annul justice nor general ethics, but makes the latter fully possible by incarnating it in the reality of human existence. As the guiding norm of Christian morals it supplants case-study with the situation. It appeals to the person and his responsibility, and consequently gives concrete shape to the objective norms. Charity knows only the real, and only charity can fulfill the meaning of the real. This does not mean that one must disregard abstract norms or the transcendent laws of nature; but it does mean that we must give the norms existence in human reality. There are in the first place the universal objective norms, such as they are found in the Decalogue. Then also there are the (objective) applications of the rules to objective "cases"; e.g., what serious inconvenience is sufficient to excuse someone from the positive law of keeping holy the Sunday? And so on. But casuistry is not sufficient for concrete behavior. Here a determined decision must be made by the personal conscience, enlightened by *Christian* prudence, which in turn takes into account the general norms, and presumably also the examples of casuistry if it is up to it. But as a Christian virtue, prudence is governed especially by faith and the intuition of love, since love is not blind but clairvoyant. Nor does this mean that in certain cases the eternal laws cease to be valid, for the supreme Christian law is charity, and it always remains in force. But it does mean that there are exceptions to casuistry, or rather that casuistry does not cover and cannot cover all cases. The Christian revelation of charity as the supreme law includes the doctrine of personal responsibility, which no one can take away from me, and which I must repeatedly exercise anew in every instance. Whoever elevates charity to the supreme principle, thereby elevates liberty as a principle, and accepts the risk which is inseparably intertwined with authentic human existence.

It may therefore be rightly asked whether charity can be imposed as a *precept;* in what sense may one speak here of law? To feel for someone, as it is commonly understood, can certainly not be imposed or commanded. Does therefore what is commanded bear relationship only to the intellect and will, to an abstract, cold, "supernatural" type of love? In daily life, however, I never love anyone with my will alone; *if* I love, then *"I"* love, with the concrete totality of my person. In the parable of the good Samari-

tan we are also told that "he was moved with compassion." Love
is deeply interested in the being of the other, and shares in it by
a disinterested dedication of its own entity to the other. For this
reason the emphasis which Jesus places on the precepts of love
of God and love of neighbor signifies a breakthrough from the
juridical order and from the abstract-juridical attitude. He commanded what no man could or would dare command.

From this it does not follow that the juridical aspect finds
no place in Christendom, and even less that the command to
love is not in earnest. It means, rather, that the juridical attitude
is really not the Christian one, and that the precept of love of
neighbor is not imposed in the same way as that of keeping holy
the Sunday. It is not imposed on us in the manner of some work
which we must do, nor as some feat we may attempt at will. It
is placed on us as an appeal to the heart (and "heart" is not to
be taken in a romantic or sentimental sense, but as the very ground
of our existence). The commandment of love is an appeal by
God to the creative potentiality of our heart, to our possibility to
express ourselves in the encounter of the other. God speaks to us
personally here; the text says: "You shall love" in the singular.

In its perfect state love therefore undoubtedly presupposes
rational maturity and human liberty (both of which are acquired
piecemeal precisely by the exercise of a still imperfect love). And
even he who possesses such maturity must still frequently be
satisfied with only an honest effort. This means that comparatively
few are capable of a full expression of love. But this again does
not mean that the precept of love is not meaningful to the rest.
Even though I am not able to realize charity fully, as man and
as a Christian I can nonetheless by my deliberate choice elect
charity as my course and my goal, as the condition of existence
which I freely accept as my own. For this reason it can be categorically imposed upon all as a precept by God, and not by man,
since God can rightfully address Himself to me in my inmost
being, and by His grace does so efficiently. Because in my efforts
at exercising charity I constantly meet with my inabilities and my
limitations, I experience myself to be a sinful creature. Even to

grasp this is, speaking as a Christian, supremely salutary. Charity is at the same time the school of humility. "Loving humility is a power, the strongest of all, and there is nothing that approaches its power" (Dostoyevsky). People with *faith,* no matter where they may be in the world, have always known this.

If a person wants to start with the old division, according to which life can be considered as a combination of relationships toward God, toward man, and toward one's self, he can find the Christian picture of these three relationships in three beautiful parables of Luke's Gospel. The relationship of man toward the heavenly Father is delineated, as has already been explained, in the parable of the prodigal son (15:11–32); that toward our neighbor, in the parable of the good Samaritan (10:25–37). How the Christian must behave toward himself (and at the same time toward God) is taught us in the brief parable of the Pharisee and the Publican. "But He spoke this parable also to some who trusted in themselves as being just and despised others. Two men went up to the temple to pray, the one a Pharisee and the other a Publican. The Pharisee stood and began to pray thus within himself: 'O God, I thank thee that I am not like the rest of men, robbers, dishonest, adulterers, or even like this Publican. I fast twice a week; I pay tithes of all that I possess.' But the Publican, standing afar off, would not so much as lift up his eyes to heaven, but kept striking his breast, saying, 'O God, be merciful to me the sinner!' I tell you this man went back to his home justified rather than the other" (18:9–14).

A man can truly humiliate himself only before the face of God, as is done in an exemplary fashion in this parable. He cannot humiliate himself before a fellow man, except and only so far as the latter represents God, which properly speaking is possible only in the sacramental order of the Incarnation. This parable is the human counterpart of the one on the prodigal son, where, as has already been noted, the behavior of the father, who represents God, occupies the center of our attention. Here the emphasis is placed on the behavior of sinful man toward God. Strictly speaking, this parable does not treat of the "relationship toward oneself," because a man is not inclined to an autonomous relationship toward himself; he is essentially directed to something outside himself, toward another. It shows us again the relationship toward God wherein man experiences himself to be a sinner; and this in simple truth without fear or anxiety. In this honest acceptance of himself he discovers deliverance from his sins and freedom from the burden of excessive demands which he would impose on himself because of distorted idealization or idolization of self. Consequently, he also goes to his home justified, exulting, but not exalting, with his head erect and lifted up by God. Because he acknowledged his uncleanness in the sight of God, he is purified, and thus enabled to enter the path of love for another. Love for one's neighbor cannot exist without humility of a type which opens us toward our fellow men because we accept our own smallness, thereby acquiring a certain innate dignity, and finding favor with God.

FIVE

Self-denial according
to the Gospels

WHOEVER SETS HIMSELF to write on self-denial and mortification enters a realm having immediate relationship with Christian conduct, and particularly with the Catholic mode of life. As far as I am able to ascertain, these subjects occupy a lesser place in Protestant thought and determine the religious life of the typical non-Catholic to a lesser degree. Among Catholics generally speaking, on the contrary, mortification is not so much a subject of theological speculation as an imperative that is accepted without much reflection. To mortify oneself by sacrifice and denial is part and parcel of normal Catholic training. Far-reaching self-renunciation is considered a necessary element of authentic Catholic life. It is given attention in seminaries, novitiates and retreat-houses. Undoubtedly, when measured by customary standards, there are many unmortified members among us; but precisely as Catholics, they in turn feel themselves to be members of lower standing. A motley quantity of motives and customs has grouped itself around the theme of mortification in the somewhat confusing copiousness of Catholic life. Even the terminology is no longer clear. Such terms as asceticism, self-denial, mortification, sacrifice, self-control, penance are often used as synonyms. They seem to be joined together in the vague consciousness of the majority by the imaginative picture of someone refusing pleasant and agreeable things because of one or another religious or ennobling motive. Therefore there is a question, mainly, though not exclusively, of the *bona delectibilia,* the delightful things of life. Of the ancient couplet, *"Abstine et sustine:* Abstain and persevere," the first has developed into the Catholic notion of mortification, which is generally considered an active denial of some legitimate pleasure, whereas the more "passive" toleration and sustaining of suffering and adversity may be considered as an oblation one brings, as a cross one is willing to bear in company with Jesus.

In the second instance we are quickly and clearly on authentic Christian footing. The acceptance of the "cross" in honor of our Lord in union with His body, the Church, is a characteristic attitude not to be found outside Christendom. The evaluation of deliberate, self-imposed renunciation of what is pleasant and desirable, as also the self-infliction of pain, hunger, thirst, privation, etc.—in short, judgment of those things which are generally classed as deliberate corporal mortification is not so simple. All sorts of motives of basically different character can be intertwined here: normal self-control, Stoic self-sufficiency, Gnostic (Manichean, Puritanic) fear and aversion of whatever is material, Christian love, and many other things.

Because psychology teaches us that the real motives of our acts are often entirely or partially "unknown," we find here an extensive and important realm for the concrete formation of consciences and the direction of souls. That, however, will not be the subject matter of this chapter. We are here interested exclusively in the objective meaning and significance of the topic as it is described in the Synoptic Gospels.

Concerning at least the terminology, we must distinguish between self-denial and mortification. The oldest Gospels deal with the first in only a few, but very important, passages; the second is treated by St. Paul, whose doctrine will be considered in the second section of this book. Because the topic of self-denial has such an eminently practical aspect, it is useful once again to point out the meaning which the Catholic ascribes to biblical doctrine.

In the first place we must be mindful that on this point, as on so many others, the Scriptures do not offer a systematic development. Our consideration is based on only a few words of the Master which were spoken in a definite historical situation and, like most logia, are aphoristic, terse, and often possess an element of paradox. They are not cautiously phrased formulas or balanced statements, carefully weighing the different aspects of a particular theme against each other. They are rather suggestive pictures whose variable meaning cannot be exhausted by just one rational explanation. They are axiomatic sayings intended to arouse consternation and dismay, sparks that will enkindle an immense conflagration. On the one hand we are obliged to take them in their historical situation; on the other hand our exegesis must remain open and take into account the atemporal character and (polyvalent) meaning of these sayings which each age must apply to itself anew. And constantly there is the danger that while we are unavoidably systematizing we clandestinely introduce our own imagery into a foreign context.

In the second place, a Catholic accepts the Scriptures in the sacred dimension of the Church; he is not confronted with it as with an individual person, as it were face to face, to find there —and there alone—the revealing God and respond by faith. He already believes, he is part of the community of the Church, he does not approach the Book alone. The Scriptures are entrusted by God to the Church, and to us all so far as we are members of the Church, children of the Church. This does not mean that the Bible acquires its authority from the Church. It is the word of God, spoken to the Church, given to the Church. The Church is the *alma mater* who feeds the believer with the word of God in the Scriptures. And she does this preeminently by her liturgy. With the supporting help of the Spirit she is the one who interprets the Scriptures with authority, and in extreme and critical cases even does so with her supreme and universally binding authority.

That the Church can interpret the Bible in this wise does not mean that the believer has no other obligation than to listen to her authoritative (and in some cases definitive) explanation.

We are parts of the Church, and the teaching power of the Church, no less than her ruling power, cannot work in a vacuum; the active cooperation of the faithful is necessary. It is within the limits of this divinely constituted authority and with a ready spirit of obedience, but not of passivity, that we are happy to listen even personally to the word of God. It is in this sense that we ask the Bible for the meaning of Christian self-denial. "For the word of God is living and efficient and keener than any two-edged sword, . . . and a discerner of the thoughts and the intentions of the heart" (Heb. 4:12). "Discerner," or arbiter; the Greek has *kritikos.* That is the leading role of the Bible. As Christians, we must subject our notions and practices to the discernment of the Scriptures; whatever is contrary to them is (objectively) not Christian. The Scriptures have the decisive, the original word, though not the only nor the last one, since the Catholic believes in the divine tradition and in the authority of the Church as the interpreter of God's word. Christian self-denial is an authentic Christian creation [1] which dates back to Christ himself. The foundation and original motivation are found in the Gospels. The Christian edifice with its rich tradition is built up on this, "for other foundation no one can lay, but that which has been laid, which is Christ Jesus" (I Cor. 3:11).

The leading text on self-denial is Mark 8:34–38 (and various parallel passages and doublets in Matthew and Luke). It reads as follows: "And calling the crowd together with His disciples, He said to them: "If anyone wishes to come after Me, let him deny himself, and take up his cross, and follow Me. For he who would save his life will lose it; but he who loses his life for My sake and for the Gospel's sake will save it. For what does it profit a man, if he gain the whole world, but suffer the loss of his own soul? Or what will a man give in exchange for his soul? For whoever is ashamed of Me and of My words in this adulter-

---

[1] When commenting on Matt. 19:28, St. Jerome observes: "He did not say only: 'You who have left all things'; Crates the philosopher did the same, and many others despised riches; but he added: 'and followed Me' because this is the hallmark of the apostles and the faithful."

ous [2] and sinful generation, of him will the Son of Man also be ashamed when he comes with the holy angels in the glory of his Father."

These words have a sharper ring than the Sermon on the Mount (although the beatitudes also tell of persecutions and, rightly understood, demand supreme self-denial); sharper, too, than many of the parables. All three evangelists insert them in a different situation and at a later period. The confession of Peter at Caesarea Philippi has already taken place; the disciples have acknowledged that in Jesus the kingdom of God has come (Mark 8:27–30). Their separation from the common crowd has become more pronounced, as also has the opposition of the leaders. Dark clouds are gathering, the crisis is coming, the decisive point cannot be far distant. Our Lord speaks of it for the first time and finds that even His disciples do not comprehend (Mark 8:31–33). It is in this grave situation that He proclaims the words on self-denial and the cross. Where the beatitudes rang alluringly and enticingly with their promises of happiness, these logia proclaim frankly what difficult conditions are demanded of all who would become true disciples. To follow Jesus has become a matter of life and death; everyone must know what fidelity to such a Master can entail. But whoever is ready to give everything shall also obtain everything. And thus, as a final conclusion, we note that even here happiness is held in prospect, and we are again in the milieu of the beatitudes.

It is evident that the whole passage belongs to the context of witnessing to or denying Christ, of our relationship to Him, of martyrdom. There is question here, if you will, of an extreme, a limit-situation. The Greek term which we translate as "deny" literally means to disavow, to negate, to say "no." The contrary is to profess, to acknowledge, to say "yes." The implication of this contrast becomes evident, once we note that alongside and opposite to "denying oneself" it says "to deny Christ," "not to confess Christ before men, to be ashamed of Him and His words" (Mark

[2] An Old Testament figure of speech, meaning: fallen away from God, idolatrous.

8:38; 10:33; 14:30; Luke 12:9). From this it follows that evangelical self-denial in its original meaning is not directed toward man himself, toward the perfection, the purification and the mastering of his own person as its proper goal, but that it is directed entirely toward Christ and the witness concerning Him. The sweeping "no" to oneself finds its meaning in the "yes" which one says to Christ by following Him. That this total giving-up of oneself is radical in principle is apparent also from the words which are added: "to take up one's cross." The disciples must be ready, if God so demands, to follow the example of their Master even to the extent of accepting and sharing His violent death. The same thought is reiterated in the following verse which speaks explicitly about martyrdom: "Who loses his life for My sake and for the Gospel's sake will save it."

The motivation (which is always the determining force in a moral act) of self-denial is entirely positive: for the sake of Christ and the Gospel, for the promulgation of God's dominion which has come in Christ. The question is not primarily one of self-control or personal formation. Granted that these are not excluded, granted that one ought perhaps even say that in the present order of original sin and redemption they can be fully achieved only by means of true self-denial, they are nonetheless not the determining motif. The formation of one's personality on a purely human level can indeed have some significance as a motive for self-denial. But if one wishes to speak of Christian self-denial then such a motivation must be incorporated into the whole of Christian existence and subordinated to it.[3] It cannot be denied that saints such as Francis of Assisi and Francis Xavier have achieved a high perfection of their human nature along the path of self-denial. But what drew them and urged them on was love for God and neighbor; the development of their personality was a by-product that was added to their exclusive search for the kingdom of God without their bothering about it. Man is not quite so autonomous that

[3] I mean, of course, among Christians. Those who err in good faith motivate their lives with noble human values, and still remain open toward that which is authentically Christian by an unconscious reference to the human perfection in Christ.

he can achieve his own perfection by deliberately striving after it.

Nietzsche's criticism of Christian morality, particularly on the doctrine of self-denial, as though this were conceived from a fear and hatred for living, is well known. The "crowd" wants to repress the vehement zest-for-life of the strong, and consequently declares "aristocratic exceptions" evil. "All the ancient moralists were univocal on this point: *Il faut tuer les passions*" (*Götterdämmerung*). Morality is the denial of the will to live! Goodness and compassion are signs of moral decay, which is afraid to live; painfully to give up one's life is the supreme mark of this decadence. This attack may have had its value for arousing a complacent Christendom before the World Wars, but our century has sadly learned to what lengths an official suspension of goodness and compassion can lead apparently normal people. The criticism of Nietzsche is surpassed and underscored by the most gruesome acts, such as he certainly would not have countenanced, but which nonetheless have been encouraged by his theories.

There is one point, however, on which it is of great importance to contradict him: Christian morality does *not* propose the destruction of one's passions. I shall go into greater detail on this matter in the second section of this book, when there is question of Paul's doctrine on mortification. Let us be satisfied here with the assertion of the obvious fact that Jesus' doctrine on self-denial, precisely as it occurs in its historical context, has nothing to do with any form of dualism within man. He is not interested in any "destruction of the passions," but in the readiness of the disciple to accept even a bloody martyr's death should the situation require this, and that out of an exceeding greatness of vital love.

More subtle than the criticism of Nietzsche is that of J. D. Bierens de Haan. It does not have the nature of an attack, but is rather an attempt to incorporate the logia of Jesus into the system of an autonomous, idealistic ethic.[4] He distinguishes the "experimental ego" from the "profound ego" or the better self.[5] Self-

[4] *Ethica: Beginselen van het zedelijk zelfbewustzijn,* Ben Haag, 1942, pp. 73–83.
[5] This latter term must not be taken in a Freudian sense, but as the nobler and more profound self.

denial, in consequence, does not mean "a crushing condemnation of our experimental-ego, but its utilization by our better self and the purification of our human nature. Hence, self-denial differs only slightly from self-restraint." The main thing is that our better self (our "nobler awareness") finds reality in the given "soul-material."

One may call to mind here the artist who at the expense of comfort and well-being consecrates himself to the actualization of his deepest artistic capabilities; or the example given by Bierens de Haan himself of the girl who renounces a fashionable life in order to achieve her ideal of some humanitarian goal. The core of one's personality, the spirit, love, is liberated; one "saves" oneself. In this line of thought it is important that the effort remains positive, and that the conclusion is not conceived negatively. Privation is accepted as inseparably connected with the ideal, but it is not looked upon as something desirable in itself.

It is truly remarkable that in his keen analysis of the logia of the Lord, Bierens de Haan not so much as mentions the underlying evangelical motif. This is indeed worthy of note, though not really to be wondered at, since in his autonomous ethics there is no room "for My sake and for the Gospel's sake." However, by such suppression one does not give evangelical self-denial its correct perspective. It gets its proper meaning only through this incentive. It is not autonomous in the sense that it will find its *ultimate* norm in the proper "self," even though this may appear as the "better self." Here it should be noted that Christian self-denial, and Christian morality in general, may not therefore be called completely "heteronomous." Our standards are not simply *outside* ourselves, they coincide with the divine design for man. One might say that through the Incarnation, ethics became more human and less heteronomous. To live and suffer for the sake of Christ and the Gospel means to live for man, since the Gospel is nothing else than the annunciation that God wants to save us all in Christ, who is the new Man and the second Adam. But it does not mean to live for myself alone and not for another. My better self is actualized only through love.

Against what is Christian self-denial really directed? What is its subject matter? Where does it preferably seek its substance? It is not directed primarily against the earthy, or sensual, or any particular class of passions, but against "oneself," against one's own person. I myself am both subject and object of my self-denial. And yet it is not I as such, but only so far as "I" stand in the way of witness for Christ and the Gospel; so far as I refuse to surrender myself to the concrete demands of the kingdom of God. It has reference therefore to selfishness in the most basic sense of the word, and not to some abstract condition which is always present within me and against which I must strive in season and out of season. It has reference to my selfishness here and now, so far as my choice in this particular situation wants to say "no" to the will of God. Self-denial must not be associated with hatred of self or even a lust for destroying, subduing, or humiliating self, such as has frequently occurred in the history of religion. It is for this reason that the matter or the object of self-denial is undefined and is determined in each particular situation only by my choice. It can be everything, anything, which in any particular situation I want to dispose of by myself, everything in which I want to be independent, whether this be in matters of sex, of finances and economics, of authority, or in the more "spiritual" realm of religion and morality. And yet it does not apply to any one particular "good" *a fortiori*. What selfishness always does include is the refusal to make oneself available for the sake of Christ and the Gospel. It is not a question of specific material goods, unless these are recognized *in concreto* by a decision of faith as obstacles to the bearing of witness.

Those whom Christ primarily addressed with these grave words were, of course, the apostles and the disciples in the strict sense of the term—those who during His earthly life wished to associate themselves with Him in complete readiness to share His lot. But the evangelists let it be known clearly that the invitation is here extended to all true Christians. Jesus did not call to Himself the disciples, but the "crowd" at large, and said to them: "If anyone (no matter who) wishes to come after Me." Luke (9:23) speaks of a "daily" taking up of the cross, thus indicating that among Christians self-denial must be present as a permanent and basic disposition of the soul. Undoubtedly one may observe with Bierens de Haan that these words were spoken by the Master in an "unusual circumstance," at the moment that the crisis of his own life was ominously approaching.[6]

God rarely calls on Christians to give testimony with their blood, although it is in this manner that these logia are accomplished in their ultimate and most profound sense. (For this reason it seems desirable not to apply these tremendous words to situations that are somewhat commonplace.) Perhaps it would be better to speak about a "border-line" situation. For Christian life is by its nature on the border and in a crisis. The perspective of martyrdom is not exceptional, but normal; it is indeed an extreme border, a termination, but not a deviation. And this is precisely the heart of the message of the Synoptic Gospels: through the word and person of Jesus, God's sovereignty erupts into our world, and whoever accepts the message puts himself and his whole life under the judgment and grace of God. Authentic Christian life means to place one's life under the standard of the cross of Christ. These words are meant for all Christians, since the invitation and the word of Christ live on in the Church, and set each one of us face to face with a decisive choice, constantly calling us from the temptations of this world, in order to engage us in the service of God's sovereignty. Although the concrete circumstances in which the Christian must fulfill his vocation as a follower of Christ may greatly change in the course of time, the situation of the Gospel is universally exemplary. And it remains the norm because Christ proclaimed it with His own words, even more, because by His life and death He incarnated it. "For the Son of Man has not come to be served but to serve, and to give His life as a ransom for many" (Mark 10:45).

The martyr in the full sense of the term, the witness in blood, fulfills these logia completely. Martyrdom is the maximum testimony before the forum of the world, the greatest love and the

[6] *Op. cit.,* p. 78.

supreme sacrifice of self. "You will be brought before governors and kings for My sake, for a witness to them and to the Gentiles" (Matt. 10:18). In the description of Jesus' blessed death the Scriptures give us the prototype and model of the Christian martyr, who even now tastes the future glory and already shares the glory of the Parousia by his going out of this world (Acts 7:54–60). In analogy this applies to the worker who in obedience to the word of God which the Church speaks to him strives to keep his Christian marriage pure, and because of this is perhaps mocked, and must surely say "no" to himself in many things; this worker, too, witnesses Christ. So also the Carmelite nun in the seclusion of her cell, seen by no one except the heavenly Father, as she fulfills the difficult state of life she has freely chosen and thus cooperates in the sublime testimony to Christ which her Order holds forth to the world, is such a self-denying witness. By its nature Christian self-denial possesses value for witnessing and recruiting power. Whether a specific act is noticed by others or not, it is always transcendent, rising above itself to point to Christ, giving testimony to the world. It does not lock a man within himself nor abandon him to himself. By it I am able to transcend my experimental ego and pass beyond my limitations. It may be compared to the hidden side of love, which receives all its splendor from love; without it, love is not real in any era when the sovereignty of God suffers opposition. Christian self-denial is every deed by which I deny myself something out of real love for a real man.

The motives which appear most commonly among our people seem to me to be these two: the need for self-control ("A child must learn to deny itself something") and the notion of having to do something extra for the sake of religion. As far as the first is concerned, it has been shown sufficiently by what has already been said that this motive is not expressly biblical, but neither does it necessarily conflict with the Scriptures. A man is naturally obliged often to refuse something which is pleasing to him and to undertake something which causes pain or costs effort. That is the story of life, which constantly confronts us with a choice of one sort or other. The real question is the attitude which I as a man and as a Christian take toward abnegation in my particular situation. And this in turn depends on the view which I hold of myself as a man and as a Christian in my world.

Whoever realizes that in his bodily and sexual inclination he must see an adversary of his soul and salvation, or at least a mode of life which he must gradually transcend by his spirit, will find sufficient reasons within himself to "mortify" his flesh. And whoever sees things in this light, *in suo sensu abundet,* more power to him! Marcel says that a man is actually to a great extent what he thinks himself to be. But when we come to study St. Paul's doctrine, it will become evident that such a view of man cannot really base itself on the Bible. Whoever, on the contrary, thinks that as a person he lives in the world in and because of his body and thus constructs his own world and makes associations with others accordingly, will never be able to strive meaningfully against his own bodily inclinations. He simply cannot understand mortification because in his view he is well-integrated in his corporeal-spiritual unity. But if he is a Christian he will be able to discover a supremely meaningful self-denial in the direction which by his choice and resolve he gives to his actions, to his being together with others in this world because of his body. He will not want his own development and his existence to be entirely autonomous, but will make them subservient to the message of God's kingdom, subservient to Christ and man.

I would rather leave to specialists the question whether to begin training toward self-control early in life. In my opinion, however, it seems that in this matter there is more offense in excess than in defect. In conformity with its original meaning, I would prefer to leave the term "ascetics" to *special* forms and methods of the spiritual life, and not use it as a designation for common, basic Christian self-denial. *Askēsis* calls to mind the image of certain special, even professional exercises, having as their purpose the acquisition of a dignity above the ordinary. When speaking of the little child, making efforts to set its first faltering steps, we do not say that it is in training. Training, furthermore, has meaning only as a means to an end; finger exercises for someone who does not intend becoming a pianist are absurd. In like manner, asceticism has its proper place in a religious context —the novice of a strict religious order, for example, who wishes to acquire that particular ability required for the facile and constant exercise of religious obedience, poverty, silence, etc. But experience shows that to attempt to change accepted usage is vain and futile.

The other popular motive for self-denial, which is popularly referred to as "wanting to do something special for our dear Lord," is closer to the motives of the Gospel, except that it is slightly tinged with legalism. One really cannot do anything "extra" for Him for whom one must do everything, for Him who has His servants declare even after they have served Him faithfully: "We are unprofitable servants" (Luke 7:10). Furthermore, just what does it mean to "do something for Christ"? What can I do for Him who has been glorified and is no longer of this world? Two things (or really only one): I can proclaim His name on earth and love those who belong to Him. "As long as you did it for one of these, the least of My brethren, you did it for Me" (Matt. 25:40). We always end up with love of neighbor. All Christian roads lead to this point. For even the preaching of the Gospel and the witnessing for Christ through the liturgy and the sacraments, through work and joy, in suffering and death are done for man; for Christ, granted, but He is inseparable from His own. And all belong to Him, Christians (the real ones) in the first place, but also all others. For God wants all men to be saved, and they will be saved only in Him; and man, every man, carries within himself the image of God, thus also of Christ, who is the perfect image of God.

It was said above that no particular "good" considered in itself must as such necessarily be given up for the sake of self-denial, but that all this depends upon one's choice in a particular situation. This does not exclude the possibility in our present *condition humaine* that some things will more easily and more generally become a hindrance to good witnessing than others. As one examines the words of Jesus in the older Gospels one finds that our Lord foresaw a danger, not indeed in the sexual but in the financial domain.[7] He has no good word for riches, except that it is the stuff one ought to get rid of as quickly as possible. Of the many texts on the subject it will suffice to transcribe one here. After the rich young man had sorrowfully departed from Jesus because "he had great possessions," the Master looked around (as is noted by Mark, who always sees everything happening) and "said to His disciples: 'How hard will it be for those who have riches to enter the kingdom of God.' And the disciples were amazed at His words.[8] But Jesus said to them again: 'Children, how hard it is to enter the kingdom of God.[9] It is easier for a camel to go through the eye of a needle than for a rich man to enter the kingdom of God.' And they were exceedingly astonished, and said to Him, 'Then who can be saved?' Jesus looked at them and said: 'With men it is impossible, but not with God; for all things are possible with God' " (Mark 10:23-27). It is therefore possible that

[7] There are many texts, especially in Luke, who, to judge from Acts (2:44, 45; 4:32), had great regard for the early Christian disdain of wealth. Cf. Luke 6:20, 24 (cf. Matt. 5:3); 12:16-21, 33-34; 14:28-33; 16:9-13; 18:18-30. But the basic passage which was treated extensively above is common to all three Gospels.

[8] Both the Old Testament and Judaism considered wealth as an unequivocal blessing from heaven. This was at least the dominant view, which was coupled with manifold exhortations toward liberality. There were also various exceptions. Thus, Koheleth remarks that all things are transitory; and Sirach 31:5 urges moderation of one's appetites. Philo's criticism of wealth is philosophically inspiring. The Essenes and/or the sect of the recently discovered Dead Sea Scrolls practiced a far-reaching community of goods. But the dominant spiritual tendencies of Judaism, which have propagated themselves in the Talmud, testify to a favorable outlook on material well-being.

[9] *Revised Standard Version*, New York, 1952. This is true in general; but as the context indicates, it is particularly applicable to the wealthy. Many manuscripts add a mitigating note: "for those who trust in riches," but this variant does not represent the original. (This is also the reading accepted by the Vulgate and by the Confraternity Version. It is incorporated into his Greek text by Merk, *Novum Testamentum—Graece et Latine,* Rome, 1944; but not by Nestle, *Greek New Testament,* New York. Trans.)

a rich man is spared, but only through a special grace from God. The real reason for this quasi-impossibility is given us in another logia: "No man can serve two masters; for either he will hate the one and love the other, or else he will stand by one and despise the other. You cannot serve God and mammon" (Matt. 6:24; Luke 16:13). Money quickly becomes a demon who lays claim on the heart and makes it insensitive for any other thing. Luke emphasized this foolishness by relating the parables of the rich farmer and the wealthy miser (12:16–21; 16:19–31).

It is not entirely impossible that the strong accent on the dangers of wealth was aimed at certain social attitudes. The Synoptic logia are to a large extent directed at a rural populace, who hardly ever take questions of money and property lightly, Not a single one of these warnings is found in the fourth Gospel. St. Paul, writing mostly to people living in Hellenic cities, sees in immorality and idolatry dangers equally as great as in avarice, but seems to consider even the last as a sort of idolatrous cult, as a worship of mammon (cf. Col. 3:5). And later on we read again: "For covetousness is the root of all evils" (I Tim. 6:10). There can be no doubt that in all strata of human society avarice is an insuperable obstacle to true Christian life. Our heart must remain free from greed in order to be open to God and to our fellow man. Christian self-denial is a happy mixture of love and spiritual freedom.

SIX

Serenity of Soul

As we now approach the conclusion of our incomplete and somewhat unsystematic reflections on "Synoptic piety" we revert to our starting point, to the revelation of God which Jesus bought in word and work, by His life and death, by His entire personality. Nowhere are these found in purer form than in the logia of the oldest Gospels. The sayings of the Lord which we read in John have a like authority, and Paul's struggle to express what moves him so deeply gives us an interpretation, equally inspired by the Spirit, of the facts of the salvation that has come in Christ. But the basic source, the clear spring, the early beginning, the sound of the voice, the flash of the eye, the inimitable reality of literal formulas, the landscape and in fact the whole milieu, the situation, the authentic and unrepeatable life, the unerring mark of authenticity—all this is found time and again in Matthew, Mark and Luke. Here we meet the reality of the Incarnation: the birds and the flowers, the children, the sea and the desert, storm and calm, activity and rest, the milling crowd and the solitude of the night, the strong compassion for the sick and the poor, the enchantment of the captivating words. "And all spoke well of Him and wondered at the gracious words that proceeded from His mouth" (Luke 4:22; *Revised Standard Version*).

The idyll of Renan is unreal and studiously one-sided.[1] There

[1] "The beautiful climate of Galilee made the existence of these unpretending

was no earthly paradise on the shores of the Sea of Galilee, the fishermen were neither angels nor dolts, and Jesus' preaching was so far from being what they in their minds and hearts had expected that even His most intimate friends did not really understand Him, and the leaders of the people opposed Him with growing success from the very beginning. A picture of the Master which lacks the perspective of strife and suffering misses character and truth. Even at the time of His first appearance in Galilee, Jesus was conscious of the background of sin and malice that are part of every man and prove to be the great obstacle for the message of God's dominion (cf. Matt. 11:20–24). He foresaw His death and accepted it as an oblation "for the ransom of many" (Mark 10:45). But it remains true nonetheless that His words, though they harbor no illusions about man, suggest the paradise which would be our common lot without shedding of blood or terror, provided only that His listeners, including ourselves, had accepted His teaching and put it into practice. And yet the powerful of this world did not want to do so, as they never do. The cross and death have become inevitable; the kingdom of God suffers violence, and paradise will come, but not without suffering and bitter strife. Now the kingdom will be given only to the "little flock," to the "poor" and the "laborer" and the "meek," who bear their burdens patiently.

"And He came to Nazareth, where He had been brought up; and according to His custom, He entered the synagogue on the Sabbath and stood up to read. And the volume of Isaias the prophet was handed to Him. And after He opened the volume, He found the place where it was written: 'The spirit of the Lord is upon me; because He had anointed me; to bring good news to the poor He has sent me, to proclaim to the captives release, the

---

fishermen an endless enchantment. Being simple, good, happy, they had a foretaste of the kingdom of God as they rolled gently on their delightful little sea, or rested on its shores in the evening. It is hard to portray the enchantment of a life which is spent thus under the open heaven, the sweet and strong love which derives from such perpetual contact with nature. . . . Occasionally there might be a naïve doubt, or lingering skepticism, but Jesus dispelled the objection with a smile or a glance."

sight to the blind; to set at liberty the oppressed, to proclaim the acceptable year of the Lord, and the day of recompense.' And closing the volume He gave it back to the attendant and sat down. And the eyes of all in the synagogue were gazing on Him. But He began to say to them: 'Today this Scripture has been fulfilled in your hearing'" (Luke 4:16–21).

What was foretold by the prophet (Isa. 61:1, 2) became reality in Jesus and continues to become reality wherever His word is believed. Indeed, the years just past have taught us to penetrate the meaning of the message of salvation for the captives and the oppressed.

In one passage in the Gospels of Matthew and Luke we can read how the Master in a single flash sees the heavenly reality of this kingdom of the poor and the humble: "In that hour He rejoiced in the Holy Spirit and said, 'I praise Thee, Father, Lord of heaven and earth, that Thou didst hide these things from the wise and prudent and didst reveal them to little ones. Yes Father, for such was Thy good pleasure. All things have been delivered to Me by the Father; and no one knows who the Son is except the Father, and who the Father is except the Son, and him to whom the Son chooses to reveal Him'" (Luke 10:21, 22; cf. Matt. 11:25–27). And Luke adds immediately: "And turning to His disciples He said: 'Blessed are the eyes that see what you see! For I say to you, many prophets and kings have desired to see what you see, and they have not seen it; and to hear what you hear, and they have not heard it'" (vv. 23, 24). God revealed Himself to Jesus, and the kingdom has already come for whoever believes in Him. In Matthew the text continues as follows: "Come to Me, all you who labor and are burdened, and I will give you rest. Take My yoke upon you, and learn from Me, for I am meek and humble of heart; and you will find rest for your souls. For My yoke is easy, and My burden light" (Matt. 11:28–30).

Whoever sits at Jesus' feet as a disciple, finds peace and comfort for his soul. He is modest, lacking all haughtiness, because He is "meek and humble of heart." With these words He contrasts Himself deliberately and expressly with contemporary Jewish scribes. Already in the Old Testament the Law, the way of life established by God Himself, is called a "yoke" (Jer. 5:5, etc.). The contemporaries of Jesus applied such expressions as the "yoke and the Law" to God's sovereignty and to the commandments and meant not only the keeping of the Torah but also all the Pharisaic customs. It had become a burdensome and oppressive yoke. The many prescriptions concerning ritual purity, for instance, and the complex casuistry with its innumerable subtleties could not possibly be remembered by the common people, let alone be observed; they felt themselves "saddled" with the Law and the traditions of the fathers, a burden they simply could not bear and without which they thought they could gain admittance neither to God nor his kingdom. The scribes were mostly inflexible in their demands, and frequently looked with contempt on the common, uneducated masses (cf. John 7:49). The first (and most severe) reproach that Jesus levels at them in the denunciation of Matt. 23 refers to this posture: "They bind together heavy and oppressive burdens, and lay them on men's shoulders; but not with one finger of their own do they choose to move them" (v. 4). By saying this, Jesus contrasts His own doctrine and His own attitude as teacher. He opposes this not only to historical pharisaism, but He rejects all haughty widsom and every unsympathetic idealism which is unwilling to admit the weakness of man. An ecclesiastical or sacerdotal word which discourages men is not in accord with His spirit. His yoke is easy and His burden light, but not because He demands less than the scribes; the surrender of heart which He demands exceeds all legal prescriptions, and the Christian has no Torah to provide security against the unlimited risks of love. His teaching is easy to bear because it grants the simple a unique revelation, the knowledge of the Father and the Son, and because He who proclaims it is Himself meek and humble.

As we have already noted when treating the Sermon on the Mount, the fascination which radiates from these solemn demands finds its ultimate ground in the person of the Master. They constitute a living morality which has become incarnate in Jesus and finds its source in the infinite authority of the Son. This authority is not pedantic, but personal, and consequently is not only "above" us, but appeals to us and attracts us in a mysterious manner. Thus the Master may rightly apply to Himself the invitation of ancient Jewish wisdom as it goes about seeking disciples: "Come to Me all. . . . Take up My yoke." [2] But He who speaks these words is no personification; He is the Son who has become man and who has given human shape to the revelation of God.

Here a word ought also be added about the doctrine of trust in prayers of petition. *Faith* in the Synoptics is really only the concrete conviction that God is almighty and will help me here and now. It is the kind of faith that works wonders and moves mountains. It is the type of faith one finds among children and saints of faith which simply disregards all intermediate agencies and sees only God and man, a faith which moves about in the divine world with the ease of a bird floating in the air. We may compare it with trust in Providence, provided that we entirely do away with all reserve and timidity. "And they came, bringing to Him a paralytic carried by four. And since they could not bring him to Jesus because of the crowd, they stripped off the roof where He was, and, having made an opening, they let down the pallet on which the paralytic was lying. And Jesus, seeing their faith, said to the paralytic, 'Son, thy sins are forgiven thee'" (Mark 2:3–5). To the sinful woman who had anointed His feet He said: "Thy faith has saved thee; go in peace" (Luke 7:50). And to the father of the epileptic boy: "All things are possible to him who believes." At once the father of the boy cried out, and said with tears: "I do believe; help my unbelief" (Mark 9:23, 24). The disciples are still of little faith; they are concerned about their

[2] Sirach 51, 23–27: "Come to me, you who need instruction, and take your place in my school; how long will you be deprived of what you need, how long will your souls remain so sorely parched? Submit yourselves to her yoke, let your souls bear her weight; for she is close to those who seek her, and he who is in earnest finds her. See for yourselves! I labored but a little for her sake, and found great rest."

food, they are filled with anxiety when it storms on the sea, they do not really trust in God (Matt. 6:30; 8:26, etc.). Jesus tells them: "Have faith in God. Amen I say to you, whoever says to this mountain, 'Arise, and hurl thyself into the sea,' and does not waver in his heart, but believes that whatever he says will be done, it shall be done for him. Therefore I say to you, all things whatever you ask for in prayer, believe that it has been granted you,[3] and you shall have it" (Mark 11:22–24).

The Old Testament was already acquainted with confidence in God and the power of supplication. The psalms are filled with it. In Isaias we read: "And it shall come to pass, that before they call, I will hear; as they are yet speaking, I will hear" (65:24; cf. Mark 11:24). And: "In a moment of indignation have I hid My face a little while from thee, but with everlasting kindness have I had mercy on thee, said the Lord thy Redeemer" (54:8). But even here Christian revelation surpasses that given to the fathers and the prophets because God now speaks and acts through His Son. In Jesus, God's ear has become attentive to us. He is the incarnate answer to all our questions and needs. Wherever He is present, no one may vacillate; our confidence must be boundless, human-specific, even constraining and importunate. "And He told them a parable—that they must always pray and not lose heart—saying: There was a judge in a certain town who did not fear God and did not respect man. Now there was a certain widow in that town, and she kept coming to him, saying, 'Do me justice against my adversary.' And he would not for a long time. But afterwards he said within himself, 'Although I do not fear God, nor even respect man, yet because this widow bothers me, I will do her justice, lest by her continual coming she finally wear me out.'"[4] And the Lord said, "Hear what the unjust judge says; and will not God avenge His elect, who cry to Him day and night? And will He be slow to act in their case? I tell you

[3] This is the reading of the oldest manuscripts, and not: "Believe that you shall receive."

[4] The original text is more dramatic: "Otherwise she will come and even strike me in the face."

that He will avenge them quickly" (Luke 18:1–8). There is here no longer question of divine omnipotence, nor of the thought that God could change everything if He so desired, but of the absolute assurance of children that has come to us in Jesus—an assurance that simply disregards the routine course of the world. St. John rightfully calls this praying *in the name of Jesus* (14:13; 15:16, etc.), and in Matthew we read: "Where two or three are gathered together for My sake, there am I in the midst of them" (18:20).

In Jesus God has approached man in the fullness of time and on the threshold of two worlds, the oriental and the occidental. In His person He combines the Isaian picture of the servant of God who brings liberation to the captive with the image of the oriental philosopher who meekly and humbly proclaims a doctrine of hope to the enslaved and the oppressed. Liberation and comfort fuse in His word. Whoever believes in Him, whoever is not scandalized in Him but will carry his cross after Him shall find rest for his soul.

> "Behold My servant, whom I have chosen,
>   My beloved in whom My soul is well pleased:
> I will put My Spirit upon Him,
>   and He will declare judgment to the Gentiles.
> He will not wrangle, nor cry aloud,
>   neither will anyone hear His voice in the streets.
> A bruised reed He will not break,
>   and a smoking wick He will not quench,
> Till He send forth judgment unto victory;
>   and in His name will the Gentiles hope."
>
> (Matt. 12:18–21; Isa. 42:1–4)

PART TWO

The Pauline Epistles

SEVEN

Paul's Conversion

WHENEVER WE ATTEMPT to examine some of the important concepts of Pauline spirituality or the "Christian life according to the
spirit of Paul," the first thing we become aware of is the difficulty
of his letters. We miss the divine simplicity of the Gospels, and
also the effortless formulation and concrete clarity of the logia.
In the epistles of the Apostle there is much agitated struggling
and even a conscious effort at finding the exact word, a wrestling
with an angel, at which man is not always victorious. It is for this
reason that once we have succeeded in penetrating his intentions,
we find in them more of ourselves, more of our own efforts toward a Christian existence in the world and in the weakness of
our own "flesh." Most of us have become too complex for the una-
dorned, rustic simplicity of the Gospel. Paul, the urbanite, the
dialectician, agile, nervous, simultaneously keen and emotional,
writing for a social milieu that has much in common with ours,
has much to say to us. But only on condition that, like the Christians of the Reformation, we, too, are capable of creating a personal relationship to his epistles. Acquaintanceship with the first
and original interpreter of the mystery of Christ can have decisive
significance for our whole spiritual life.

To be able to understand his letters, we must first have a picture of the man Paul, an idea of his life and destiny, of his history.
In a certain sense one might even say that it is not necessary to

know the "life" of Jesus to be able to understand His words. He has given Himself entirely and directly in His words; they are the perfect expression of His essence, as they are not and cannot be for anyone else. It is true of all great thinkers and poets that their message is more important than their biography. By their words they have given suitable embodiment to their personality. It is not the anecdotes of Dante's life that have meaning and significance for us, but his *Divine Comedy;* here he lives again. His adventures interest us only as explanations of his writings. Though it is true that the epistles of Paul constitute only a minor portion of his manifold activity and are to a certain extent only a by-product of his apostolic labors, yet for us they are more important than all his other work, for us they represent the whole man in his true character. And if therefore in this chapter we recall a few events of his life in order to facilitate the understanding of his imagery, the interpretation of these events is nonetheless taken entirely from his own letters. It is not the events in themselves which are important, but the meaning they acquire from the man who experienced them.

Of the Apostle Paul most Catholics know no more than that he was born at Tarsus in Asia Minor, was educated by Gamaliel, fiercely persecuted the infant Church, was suddenly converted (*The Road to Damascus*), accomplished an incredible amount of work on his missionary journeys, and finally died a martyr's death in Rome. In this picture at least one thing is correct: it shows us a man who is intensely alive and thrusts his conviction to its ultimate consequences, no matter what they may be. But the picture contains many lacunae, the principal ones of which we can perhaps discover by asking ourselves: Just what was this *conversion?* From what did he turn away and to what did he turn?

By conversion we commonly understand a process (though not necessarily a gradual one) in the soul by which someone turns away from a sinful life and embraces a pious and virtuous existence. Paul himself later looks back on his life preceding Damascus as being worthless. Because he persecuted God's Church, he tells us, he was not worthy to be called an apostle. To him, as one born out of due time, Christ appeared last of all; only the grace of God saved him (see for example I Cor. 15:9-11). But undoubtedly even before his conversion he was a person whom we would call religious, someone who thought he was living entirely in conformity with the will of God and certainly was not consciously selfish. From his youth he had been trained in the fear of the Lord; by nature he belonged to that category of men to whom religion is the most important thing in heaven and on earth. He was, furthermore, an idealist, who consecrated himself wholeheartedly to the exigencies of the Jewish cult. When he fanatically persecuted the Church, he did so only because he was sincerely convinced that Christianity constituted a fatal menace to what he considered to be the only way to serve God. In what then did his "conversion" consist? It consists in what would be called, in Freudian terminology, the exchange of one *Über-ich* for another, an exchange as sudden as it is inexplicable. But it was also the *encounter* with a person in the strongest possible sense of this term, the encounter with Jesus who made of Paul a different person.

One can form some idea of Paul's conversion if one were to imagine that an idealistic, completely unselfish Communist were suddenly transformed into a zealous, idealistic and convinced Christian. Such a turn-about is imaginable except for the element of non-preparation and suddenness. This last element remains unaccountable also in the case of Paul. It is what we call "a miracle of grace," though that really does not help matters a bit. But he himself could not find a different expression for it. It was the omnipotent and simultaneously tender grace of God which then laid hold of him. That he experienced this suddenly and wholly as something which simply overwhelmed him while leaving him complete liberty in the conquest is evident from his own accounts (which will be considered later) of the event and from the physical and psychic reactions noted by the Acts (9:1-19).

In what then did his *Über-ich* at that time consist? Or let us make the question simpler: What was the real core of the religious-moral conviction that had determined his life till that mo-

ment? It was the Jewish religion in the specialized form of
Pharisaism, which may to a large extent be equated with the rabbinic traditions that we find in the Talmud. One must be wary
of the over-simplification that satisfies itself by identifying this
spiritual movement with religious hypocrisy. It is true that the
Pharisees are often depicted as hypocrites in the Gospels, and their
system did frequently lead to religious dishonesty. But he is sadly
mistaken who thinks that this constituted the essence of Pharisaism, and that a personality of Paul's calibre can be characterized
as deliberately dishonest in any phase of his life. Pharisaism was
an extremely serious business, and its significance extends far beyond a limited historical or local occurrence. Essentially it was
an existential religious posture of a kind which is a real possibility in any religious experience and, being what it is, consequently
embodies a menace for every religion, not barring Christianity.
The real import of Paul is that he overcame this possibility within
himself (that it was overcome in that one moment which constitutes his conversion), and that later in his preaching and in his
epistles he unmasked it and fought it when it became a danger
which threatened the Church from within.

Pharisaism was historically limited and therefore embodied
characteristics which no longer appear in a similar form at the
present time. Essentially it can be described as the heresy of religious autarchy or self-sufficiency, which must not be regarded
so much as a tendency but as a way of living and an ideal for life.
It is the unconscious but active conviction that in religious matters
one must take his destiny into his own hands. And this means
nothing less than that one can determine one's own eternal for-
tune, as also the unique meaning and tenor of one's entire life.
This is really the essence of pride as it is beautifully illustrated by
Luke, chapter 18. From this, however, it may not be concluded
that all Pharisees were actually proud. Spiritual pride was the
natural consequence of the system (and in opposing the system,
Paul radically and mercilessly draws the necessary consequences
from its principles). This was a result of the very special place
which the Torah, the Law of Moses, occupied in the system.

It is almost impossible to describe a religious movement in

a few short sentences without being unjust either toward the system or its adherents. Men are often so much better than their principles. There is much real piety in the Talmud, and the immense sufferings of the Jewish people bid us speak reverently about that which for centuries was the only support and comfort for thousands upon thousands among them. The Pharisaism to which in the time of Jesus and Paul the majority of the scribes or rabbis belonged was not the only religious tendency in Judaism, though it was the leading one. After the destruction of the temple and the holy city (in 70 A.D.) and the cessation of the official sacrifice, its influence upon the spiritual life became stronger than ever before. At any rate, the Pharisee had the Law and the Old Testament, the precepts and the prohibitions, which, as we saw above, Jesus reduced to and, as it were, personified in the two precepts of love. Between God and man there was the Law with its many precepts, which the scribes had increased, amplified, and scrutinized *ad infinitum*. Could a common man still recognize God behind all these precepts? It had been forgotten that the Law was not an end in itself but in God's intention only a means by which the Jew was to subject himself to God's will until the coming of the Messias, to the time of salvation. For the true rabbi the Torah was the acme of revelation, to which even the Messias could really not make any changes or additions. God was in the heavens; man with his liberty was here on earth. God had given the Law to the Jews as His perfect and comprehensive gift. "Through it God created the world." "Because of her, man, the world, and Israel were created" (*P. Aboth*). The relationship of man to God depended entirely on his relationship to the Law, which is to say on his own freedom. The grace of God as the indispensable means to do His will was certainly not denied theoretically, and was piously acknowledged by many in practice. But the rabbinical doctrine on man declared that he received his soul pure and holy from the hands of the Creator and that a "good intention" was of itself sufficient to curb "evil." Pharisaism really professed complete liberty *à la Sartre*, except that it was directed toward the law of God. Life was not absurd.

On this foundation there gradually grew up an extended casuistry. Every observation of a command meant "merit"; every transgression, "punishment." In heaven there was strict book-keeping of all actions. The whole point of the business was to have more merits than demerits. As long as this is the case at the time of death and of judgment, the circumcized person will be pronounced free by God, he will be "justified," and he will have achieved his "justification." God is then compelled to declare him free. It is evident that in consequence of this system the Pharisee could say that he effected his own justification by observing the commandments of God by the power of his own freedom. This was not easy. It demanded much effort and "asceticism." Even the large masses of the Jewish people (not to say anything here about pagans) were hardly capable of this simply because they could not have the required "knowledge." Besides great power of will there was required also a considerable amount of clerical knowledge.

It was therefore a religion of great moral consequence, of unlimited liberty and responsibility, of unceasing effort, of triumph and defeat, of pious accounting and the accumulation of merits and "works of the Law." But it turned out to be a system that tragically overshot its mark. "Woe to you, Scribes and Pharisees, hypocrites! because you pay tithes on mint and anice and cummin, and have left undone the weightier matters of the law, right judgment and mercy and faith" (Matt. 23:23). Even of the Old Law the proper *telos* (*finis*) was "mercy and not sacrifice"; but this was not achieved by the Pharisees, and if it was, it was in spite of their system.[1]

[1] What is the difference between the "New Law" of Christianity and the Pharisaic observance of the Law, regardless of the points where they coincide (merit, reward, punishment)? The admission that we need God's grace to do His will, and the belief that this grace is given man through Christ's cross and redemption. Personal merit is therefore regarded primarily as a fruit of God's grace. Furthermore, through the twofold commandment of love as dominating principle and *forma virtutum* the strictly legal character of the Law is annulled, and the keeping of the Law by a Christian becomes part of his personal relationship to God. Heaven itself is not something material and extensive, but a glorification of God as well as the

It was in this spiritual world that Paul lived with heart and soul. "For you have heard of my former manner of life in Judaism; . . . how I advanced in Judaism above many of my contemporaries in my nation, showing much more zeal for the traditions of my fathers" (Gal. 1:13, 14). "Circumcized the eighth day, of the race of Israel, of the tribe of Benjamin, a Hebrew of Hebrews; as regards the Law, a Pharisee; as regards zeal, a persecutor of the Church of God; as regards the justice of the Law, leading a blameless life" (Phil. 3:5-6). And it was this world which was to collapse if Christianity were to succeed. Jesus did not repeal the Law, but He fulfilled and surpassed it by His proclamation of the supremacy of love. He treated the "traditions of the Fathers" with sovereign liberty, and preferably associated with sinners and publicans, that is to say with transgressors of the Law. His followers entertained the opinion that they could share in salvation through the redemptive power of His death and by faith, and not by keeping the Law. Some of them, as for example Stephen, even went so far as triumphantly to foretell the end of the Law and of the temple. And those who held such opinions were pious Jews, not uncircumcized pagans. As long as Paul lived in his old world, considering his character, he could not do otherwise than persecute Christians unto death. "And the witnesses laid down their garments at the feet of a young man named Saul. . . . But Saul was harassing the Church; entering house after house, and dragging out men and women, he committed them to prison" (Acts 7:58; 8:3).

Concerning his own conversion Paul writes: "when it pleased God to reveal His Son in me" (Gal. 1:15). Christianity is a person, not a "thing," not even an "ideal." I can chance upon it in every person I meet. "Saul, why persecutest thou *Me?*" Paul persecuted Christians, not Jesus; it is even probable that he never even knew the Master during His earthly life. Zeal for "religion" can mislead a person to bigotry, just as it led Paul to furious fanaticism.

---

personal blessedness of man, which springs "organically" from his loving relationship to Christ. The dangers of existential "Pharisaism" can *au fond* be overcome only by the primacy of love.

But the first thing he learned on his conversion was that in religion there is really question of an inter-personal relationship. It was not a matter of the Law, but of the Son of God. A man is not justified by the "works of the Law" but by faith, that is, in virtue of one's relationship to Christ (Rom. 3:20; Gal. 2:16, etc.). This, as also the contrast contained in these words, is the core of Paulinism, and it was given (and in what an astounding manner!) in that one instant, there, before the gates of Damascus. But what about sins? They are forgiven for the sake of the same Christ who was sent by God to reconcile the world with Him on the cross. This was the great deed of God's grace, which rendered the Old Law superfluous and annulled it. And He calls *me,* Saul, to faith in Christ, and through faith to salvation; and He calls all, not only the observant and the elite, but the great mass of the Jews, even sinners and publicans—and not only the Jews but even the unclean Gentiles. And He calls me, Saul, to proclaim this message, me, the scribe and Pharisee, to preach to the Gentiles.

That which he had persecuted now appears to be the only way to salvation chosen by God, and the fulfillment, not the annulment of the Jewish religion. He whom he had despised was the Messias of the Jews and the Savior of the world. Later on he will avow: "Have I not seen Jesus our Lord?" (I Cor. 9:1); he too was a witness of the resurrection; he too was an apostle. And "Christ Jesus has laid hold of me" (Phil. 3:12). He always describes his conversion in terms of entering into relationship with Christ, of an encounter with the Lord. It was above all a seeing, presumably a seeing with his bodily eyes, but especially a spiritual seeing of Christ, a "revealing" of Christ to him. From henceforth Jesus is the focal point of his view of man and the world, and he sees all things "in Christ." At the same time conversion was for him an experiencing of the overwhelming power of God's grace: an understanding and a realistic experiencing of power at the same time. He was given the liberty of being bound in love, not naturally as some sort of static quality, but as a dynamism which drove him constantly on the way (see Phil. 3:12 ff.).

Through the encounter with Christ, Paul's conversion signified the collapse of his former world, the annihilation of his values.
This is the way he dramatically describes it many years later:
"But the things that were gain to me, these, for the sake of Christ,
I have counted loss. Nay more, I count everything loss because
of the excelling knowledge [2] of Jesus Christ, my Lord. For His
sake I have suffered the loss of all things, and I count them as
dung that I may gain Christ and be found in Him, not having
a justice of my own, which is from the Law, but that which is
from faith in Christ, the justice from God based upon faith" (Phil.
3:7–9). What had been his highest treasure—Pharisaism, the *fine
fleur* of Jewry—precisely that was taken away from him. What he
had given up was not merely money, or respect, or some sinful
relationship such as Augustine was later to do; it was his religious
ideal, the whole meaning of his life.

But the encounter with Christ gave new orientation to his
existence. His conversion was the moment of birth of a personal
relationship to the Master, such as has not found its counterpart
in the history of Christianity. This gives rise to the wonderful
expressions in his letters of the most intimate relationship of love
with Jesus, written with absolute originality, without precedent,
and never to be paralleled. "With Christ I am nailed to the cross.
It is now no longer I that live, but Christ lives in me. And the
life that I now live in the flesh, I live in the faith of the Son of God,
who loved me and gave Himself up for me" (Gal. 2:20). "For
me to live is Christ and to die is gain" (Phil. 1:21). And through
this personal relationship as the center of his religious experience
he was preserved from the great danger that was so natural to
him, fanaticism. The reality of this possibility was clearly indicated by his persecution of the Church. As a Christian, he did
not succumb to this vice again because he had learned from Christ
that one must suffer before glory will come in the next life, and
that one may readily suffer for his religion but one must not inflict
violence. The revelation of Christ was also the revelation of fellow-

---

[2] The biblical term "knowledge" frequently signifies, as it does here,
both love and personal relationship.

ship with Christ; in Jesus he met the Christians: "Saul why persecutest thou Me?" The Lord who appeared to him was one with him and through him called even the Gentiles to his flock. At Damascus the mystery of the Church was unveiled to him.

What may be called the spirituality of Paul, that is to say, the manner in which he views and experiences the possibility of a positive relationship of man to God, we find indicated succinctly but totally in his conversion as he interpreted it. It is above all a protest against Pharisaism as a continuous, wholly human potentiality for religious experience. It contains a complete acknowledgement of his own impotence and sinfulness, but also faith in the revelation of God's grace and mercy. This revelation was made by Christ's incarnation and His death on the cross. Through Jesus' death on the cross "the world is reconciled to God," which is to say that the foundation is laid on which the relationship of man to God can be re-established. Through the glorified Christ and His Spirit man is truly saved and sanctified, if he believes in the "grace" of God, which is to say, in Christ. Thus Christian life—which is a life of faith and love, a life which frees from sin and the Law, which establishes fellowship with the Church, and opens the vista of a glorious resurrection—becomes possible.

EIGHT

The Concept of Sin

THE DENIAL OF Pharisaism as a system for salvation, which Paul had realistically discovered by his conversion, consists in the destruction of self-conceit in matters of religion, in the dissolution of the great illusion that our relationship to God can be primarily determined by our own effort. "So then there is question not of him who wills nor of him who runs, but of God showing mercy" (Rom. 9:16).

This applies also to the call to Christianity, to what is theologically called the first justification. It is not therefore a matter of being born of Catholic parents or of a Catholic education, although both of these can be used by God as external but important means. Everyone is called personally by the grace of God, even those who are born and baptized as Catholics; even these, once they have reached human maturity, will be placed by God once or possibly several times in a situation of decision.

This is equally applicable to Paul's own mature Christian holiness, as is evident from what he writes in one of his later epistles: "May I gain Christ and be found in Him, not having a justice of my own, which is from the Law, but that which is from faith in Christ, the justice from God based upon faith; so that I may know Him and the power of His resurrection and the fellowship of His sufferings. . . . Not that I have already obtained this, or already have been made perfect" (Phil. 3:9–12). We must not

97

consider these words merely as an expression of Paul's personal humility (cf. I Cor. 15:9; Eph. 3:8); they refer to the Christian state as such. In the Apostle's opinion, to be a Christian is precisely to know that we owe everything to God's grace and not to our own achievement. We are not under the Law but under grace (Rom. 6:15); we are led by the Spirit, and are not subject to the sway of the Law (Gal. 5:18). This means that we are people who look to God for salvation and not to ourselves: "What hast thou that thou hast not received? And if thou hast received it, why dost thou boast as if thou hadst not received it?" (I Cor. 4:7). To be under the Law (in the radical sense of Paul's polemic) means to hold that one can obtain salvation through the effort of one's own will, that one can achieve his own sanctification at the cost of much exertion and many deeds. But this religious autarchy is doomed to absolute failure. In Rom. 7, Paul outlines the startling picture of this self-sufficiency, the image of the ambitious and proud man, such as the Apostle sees him in the light of Christian revelation. The noted passage does not describe the impotence of the well-intentioned, weak man, of the "poor drudge," but the complete moral inability of the proud man who relies on himself and not on the grace of God. Here he satirizes the "confidence in the flesh" (Phil. 3:3). Whoever relies on his own strength is victim of a great illusion. He stands under the power of sin. He has no defense against it, but does not know this because ultimately he does not want to know.

The doctrine of the Apostle Paul on sin, as he exposes it in the first half of his epistle to the Romans, is difficult to grasp for many people of our age and still more difficult to accept. Various reasons can be given for this. One of them is the vacillation of point of view which most people of our time assume, without clearly examining the reason why, whenever they speak about this matter or let their thoughts dwell on it. In Romans (on which this study is chiefly based) Paul writes about sin as a power which dominates human existence as long as it is not redeemed by Christ. Precisely because he considers it as a common lot rather than as an individual deed, he can personify it as *Hamartia,* sin, the tyrant who with the aid of the Law brings man to slavery and to death. "Through one man, sin entered into the world and through sin death" (Rom. 5:12). This dramatic figure of speech must not be understood literally, but it must be taken seriously; it expresses the fact that human existence has been affected by sin from its very beginning. Whenever Paul has in mind certain sinful actions, he prefers other terms such as "transgression," or "offence." "Sin" is generally used in the singular as the state of estrangement from God, of inability of attaining to God, as the sum total of all individual "sin," as a power that fatally dominates man whenever he withdraws himself from Christ. He does not isolate it from human responsibility, but it is in his view more than the fault of the individual. It is, as it were, already present even before the decision of the individual man; it is a sort of tragic solidarity inseparably bound up with our concrete existence. Only the grace of God, given us in Christ, can free us from it; but this liberation, though radical in principle, always remains precarious in this life, to the extent that the Christian can fall into sin because of the "flesh," which indeed is crucified in him, but never completely overcome. Thus there is, perhaps, a certain affinity between Paul's "sin" and our notion of "original sin," as long as we take the latter to mean not only the beginning and cause but also the sum of all sinful deeds.

Today's Catholic, on the contrary, generally views sin from an individualistic and psychological point of view. The chief question he asks is really this: To what extent can this act be attributed to me personally and what are its consequences for me? He sees sin as something moral rather than existential. The aspect of individual responsibility occupies the foreground. It is not necessary here to trace the reasons for this way of thinking of the occidental Catholic Christian, and it seems to me self-evident that the brief description which I have just given should not be taken as a censure. It is possible that this comparison with the Pauline outlook will reveal certain lacunae, but on the other hand the moral-theological development of the doctrine on sin has certainly had its beneficial results. Thus, current distinction between mortal and venial sin has the advantage that it accentuates the essence of sin as a deed. The same can be said of the differentiation between "material" and "formal" sin—provided one understands well these classificatory adjectives, whose signification varies from that attributed to them in many secular contexts.

Real sin (as an action) can only be that sin which is at the same time a *peccatum formale,* which is to say, an action which, *speaking concretely,* is a transgression of God's will and a real act of disobedience. It must therefore be, to express it quite simply, something worth sweating over, and an action that is done with full knowledge and deliberation, as the catechism states. It must be a real *actus humanus,* a completely human action. Generally speaking, a certain human maturity is absolutely indispensable for the concrete possibility of sin in the full sense of the word. The actual possibility of mortal sin is a consequence of man's supreme dignity, of the freedom and responsibility with which he has been endowed by God in this state of pilgrimage to his fatherland. The possibility of sin and the possibility of sanctity are situated on the same plateau, namely, that of created liberty *in statu viae.* The possibility of eternal rejection (concerning the actuality of which with respect to a particular person no revelation has ever been given) indicates that God esteems man highly and has endowed his existence with limitless dimensions. Everyone is acquainted with the words of Dante that end the inscription above the gate of hell: "Leave all hope behind, ye who enter here." Less known is the statement, equally bold and true, which precedes it: "Justice moved my supreme Maker; divine Omnipotence, supreme Wisdom and first Love, created me."

But this freedom and responsibility of man are in fact often impeded or obscured. What is frequently lacking is not so much "full knowlege" as real liberty. This need not be perfect to be able to speak of sin, since perfect freedom is seldom or never acquired here on earth. But it must be real. In cases of doubt, judgment on the actual presence of concrete freedom must be left to experts, although common sense and the normal knowledge of man (provided it is not impeded by fear) are generally competent to decide. Final judgment belongs only to God. And one may safely add that the compulsion "to decide" every instance defin- itively is unhealthy and takes no account of God's mercy and the true state of man. If indeed the conditions for a complete human act are present, then mortal sin must be considered as the greatest evil that can befall a man and even, to a certain extent, the only evil, so far as it is the cause of all other evils.

What is lacking in this outlook is the understanding of man's solidarity in sin. In spite of all the correct emphasis on personal responsibility, the danger is never excluded of viewing the matter too atomically, of paying too much attention to individual actions and to individual people, and too little to what conditions our whole existence and binds us all together. We are too greatly con- cerned with pangs of conscience and too little with the true notion of sin. We interpret our feelings of guilt as being merely personal and not sufficiently as pointing to our common condition; too little, I might almost say, in line with the archetypes of C. G. Jung. Here we can learn much about Paul's utterances on *Hamartia,* the sin of man. It is not without reason that Adam has the name he has, for it simply means *"Man,"* "Everyman." He is in us and we are in him, before we are in Christ. By our personal sins we confirm and actualize the sin of "Adam."

There is a mysterious solidarity which binds mankind to- gether in sin; and in this Christ willed to share above all, and with Him and after Him all the saints. An educated and sincere Catholic once said to me: "One cannot really call Christ man, be- cause He never sinned." To this one may naturally reply (as I did at first) that Christ assumed a real human nature and that actual sinning does not belong to the essence of human nature (as *animal rationale,* and the like). But such abstract and strictly es- sentialistic considerations satisfy only a few people any more. The real answer to the unphilosophic but nonetheless deeply felt ob- jection is given us by St. Paul when he writes: "For our sakes He made Him to be sin who knew nothing of sin, so that in Him we might become the justice of God" (II Cor. 5:21). He who never committed sin still had more to do with sin than any other man, because He took upon Himself the sins of us all. No true Christian may imagine that he can escape this solidarity even though through Christ he hopes to overcome sin. On a deeper and, as it were, on an older and more primary level than that of strict personal responsibility we are and remain allied with all sinners.

Complete victory over sin is not part of this world. Christ conquered it by His death and glorification, but the risen Savior no longer belongs to this eon. We Christians have part in His victory, but at the same time we are still living in this world and in the flesh. Christ has left us behind to continue by His power the struggle against sin with a love for all sinners, which is to say, for all men including ourselves. Those who understood Him best, the saints, many of whom, as far as we can see, led entirely blameless lives, still suffered the most because of sin; for them, and especially for them, it was not an objective given quantity in the world, but an intimate experience of their existence, something which could separate them and us all from God.

According to Paul there is indeed a qualitative difference between the just man and the sinner: "There is therefore now no condemnation for those who are in Christ Jesus" (Rom. 8:1). But Christians can lose this state of grace (see I Cor. 10:1–13; Rom. 11:17–22); they are freed from sin, but not from the possibility of sinning; and this is not an abstract but a real possibility because the "flesh" in them has indeed been overcome in principle but not completely (see Gal. 5:13–26). And no one has the absolute assurance that he is justified. Paul says of himself: "For I have nothing on my conscience, yet I am not thereby justified; but he who judges me is the Lord" (I Cor. 4:4). "For in many things we all offend" (Jas. 3:2). If the Christian perseveres to the end, he attributes this as also his first justification to the grace of God. In this life we remain bound up with sin. Whoever denies this has no idea either of his own origin or of his possibilities.

As a motto for one of his novels, Graham Greene uses this text of Péguy: "Le pécheur est au coeur même de chrétienté. . . . Nul n'est aussi compétent que le pécheur en matière de chrétienté.

Nul, si ce n'est le saint." [1] The sinner is so experienced in matters of Christianity because the God of Christians is the one who justifies the impious (Rom. 4:5). But the sinner who "is at the heart of Christianity" is the sorrowful sinner, or at least the one who is ready to acknowledge himself a sinner. Not the shallow man (since real sin is a matter of deep dimension), nor the callous, and least of all the proud. Scobie is weak and meek, and so are most of Greene's heroes; often we can apply to them what has been stated above, concerning the factors that diminish or remove the formal sinfulness of a particular deed. The "real sinner" is not like one of these. He is an egotist who is hardened in uncharitableness, whose sin consists in greed and heartlessness, in hatred or social exploitation, or in pride. The essence of sin is the posture of self-sufficiency toward God and toward one's fellow man; self-seeking in its basic meaning as in contrast to love. Does this mean that impurity is no sin, or hardly one? A ridiculous question! Lust is a grave sin of common occurrence which engenders much evil. Jesus speaks of it comparatively seldom, possibly because Jewish conditions in the Palestine of his day were quite decent in this regard, possibly because He did not consider this sin as a principal cause of evil, possibly because of both reasons. But Paul writes of it all the more because the Greco-Roman world was far from exemplary on this point. And he deals with the matter without mincing words, for example, in Rom. 1:24–27 and I Cor. 6:12–20, in which latter place one finds a truly Christian attitude toward this evil, a reflection that touches the heart of the matter, without irrelevancies and without intimidation. In this light, Kinsey's prattle about "Talmudic-Christian taboos" simply does not make sense. But impurity is not sinful because it deals in matters of sex, *in venereis,* to use the theological term, but because it is "disorderly," both as human and as Christian conduct.[2] It places the

[1] "The sinner is at the very heart of Christianity. No one is as experienced in matters Christian as is the sinner. Absolutely no one, unless it is the saint."
[2] On this point the booklet by Josef Pieper, *Zucht und Mass,* Muenchen, 1947, is highly commendable.

"ego" above Christ, which is to say, above fellow man. A sin of impurity which does not distort the dignity of man is inconceivable. Divine law is transcendent in its origin and perfection, but it is incarnated in our human reality. The element of sex specifies impurity as a certain kind of vice, differing for example from gluttony or pride, but it does not constitute its sinfulness; this arises only from the disorderliness of the deed. And then we are naturally proceeding from the supposition that in the concrete it is a free and responsible act in the manner stated above. No man who is acquainted with life will dare assert that our wounded liberty is at its best on this point. Especially not in our state of society where puritanical fear and libertine reaction both lead to the same unnatural overconsciousness. Paul expresses all this so simply: "Love does no evil to a neighbor" (Rom. 13:10) and this applies to every true love.

It has often been asked whether the Apostle's vision of sin as a universal power dominating mankind is not pessimistic, inhuman and paralyzing to human endeavor. Does it not hinder the Christian from consecrating himself whole-heartedly to his earthly task? Is it not inspired by the belief that the world will soon end? Are we not dealing here with the ethics of perdition? It is characteristic of our mental outlook that we ask first about the psychological and not the intrinsic truth of a doctrine. It is possible to think of several answers. One might point to the paradox that those who believed most strongly in the radical corruption of man, such as the (historical) Puritans and their colleagues, displayed an amazing energy and dominated the world more thoroughly than those with a more optimistic outlook on man. But the first thing that must be said here to the believing Christian is that the Apostle speaks to us in the name of God and that he supports his position of the sinfulness of man with the Sacred Scriptures of the Old Testament (see Rom. 3:10-20). The second source of his thesis is not an *a priori* assumption, but observation and experience (cf. Rom. 1:18-2:29); an experience which is unfortunately true even today. The dogma of original sin, though beyond comprehension for the intellect, fits all too well with human experience. It is difficult to deny, as Newman put it, that our race "is involved in some vast aboriginal calamity." Or, as Pascal states it: "Le péché originel est folie devant les hommes. Mais cette folie est plus sage que toute la sagesse des hommes. Car, sans cela, que dira-t-on qu'est l'homme? Tout son état depend de ce point imperceptible." [3] And Dostoyevsky observed correctly that reason is dumbfounded before the ears of an innocent child. Even more than by the out-and-out wickedness of a few individuals, the dogma of original sin is suggested by the moral mediocrity of the many and the continuous failure of the best-intentioned efforts at organizing a better world.

And yet the Christian concept of sin by no means signifies that the Christian must not strive toward bettering the earth as a dwelling place for man, and that he is not called to cooperate in God's plan for creation (cf. Gen. 1:26–31). To us has been promised a new world, where justice will dwell (II Pet. 3:13). But by faith we know that our efforts alone are not capable of bringing about this turn toward the good and that the advent of the kingdom depends solely on God's good pleasure. However, if something of ours can contribute anything, then by God's grace it is that love which advances the perfect community of the saints, the truly classless society.

For spirituality in a more narrow sense, the Pauline realization of human weakness and sinfulness in no wise represents a romantic flirtation with the faults and failures of which most of us are guilty. This realization of human weakness is precisely *not* what he himself calls an "occasion for sensuality" (Gal. 5:13). Nor is it an awareness that all of us are somewhat weak. It goes much, much deeper; it is not a psychological, but a religious-existential understanding of oneself as basically powerless (and as being supported by God's merciful grace at the very roots of one's being). This understanding is a source of great spiritual power (which is not the same as "will-power," a concept not to be bandied

[3] "Original sin is foolishness in the sight of men. But this folly is wiser than the wisdom of men. For without it, what could one say of man? His whole status depends on this delicate point."

about). It frees us from all paralyzing nervousness, and opens the way to love. This humility does not hinder our energy, but liberates it. It extricates us from a false notion of self and consequently from any doomed effort at setting ourselves up as an idol, which would subjugate our attention and effort to a phantom and withdraw them from the radiation of love. There are no virtues which ask more self-denial of the normal man than love and humility. Whoever has once seen himself in the light of God's revelation and accepted himself at his true value need not spend any time or effort on his own ego; he should use them for the truly human and Christian: the relation toward God and neighbor. And by doing so, he shall himself become "better."

Paul has been given us by God as a divine gift, as the apostle whose most personal experience consisted in realizing the moral and religious impotence of the haughty man (the rest then becomes self-evident), and simultaneously the deep sense of the omnipotence of God's grace. From this discovery of human inability and of overpowering grace comes liberty, and in this liberty love becomes possible, and this love becomes active, endlessly active, as is well illustrated in the person of Paul. "I can do all things in Him who strengthens me" (Phil. 4:13). But Paul sees this effort, this "labor" (I Thess. 1:3) as a "fruit" of the Spirit (Gal. 5:22), as something that grows spontaneously in this climate of humility and liberty; and he keeps on seeing it as a fruit of God's grace and not as a product of his own will-power.

" 'My grace is sufficient for thee, for strength is made perfect in weakness.' Gladly therefore I will glory in my infirmities, that the strength of Christ may dwell in me" (II Cor. 12:9). Whenever people are apprehensive of acknowledging their own (as well as our common) weakness, and fear that from such acknowledgment damage will result to religion, it is because, basically, they lack faith. They do not really believe, with the Apostle, in the surpassing power of God which is given us through the Spirit of Jesus. They slight God's honor.

NINE

Homo Religiosus

IN THE FIRST SECTION we discussed the notion of God which is found in the oldest Gospels, particularly in the sayings of the Lord, and we ascertained that Jesus revealed God as the Father in heaven, as the One who is both far and near, exalted and merciful. In the epistles of the Apostle we find a similar impression of God but presented in its own idiom.

Paul is filled with the majesty and glory of God, with the thought of God as the perfect and absolutely encompassing reality. This awareness of God's reality and exaltedness combined, he shares with all *homines religiosi*.[1] The feeling for the divine, the numinous, the sacred makes them what they are; like poets, they are characterized by a definite feeling for the glory in creation and the urge to capture this in the shape of words. For the religious man God is as clear as water, as evident as the air he breathes, and at the same time as exalted as the heavens. This experience is familiar to all mystics of all religions.

When we speak of an "innate feeling for the divine," we use an expression equally inadequate and obscure, as the somewhat trite expression "poetic nature." The perception of the numinous is a real possibility in the nature of man. It is possible to argue this

[1] The Latin expression is not used here as a matter of pedantry, but because, in my opinion at least, the vernacular equivalent "the religious man" too readily suggests the thought of particular religious practices.

more or less *a priori* from the Thomistic notion of man, for example. It also follows from the fact that far and away the majority of people seemed to be approachable on this point, at least they were so up to our day. Whether our technical culture is busily forming another type of man, who will be not only post-church and post-Christian, but also post-religious, for whom God is really dead (to use Nietzsche's expression, "stone-dead"), is a question which need not be answered here. According to some analysts, this is not the case; even the person who has not been going to church for generations is not completely *a-religious*. In this connection one may point to the tenacity with which religion is able to persist in the most unfavorable circumstances and to the fact that convinced atheists not infrequently devote themselves to their ideals with a truly religious zeal. Whatever the case may be, it is not this common human disposition for matters religious which characterizes the *homo religiosus,* just as the artist possesses more than that great or lesser sense for beauty which is common to all. What separates the mystic from the crowd is the spontaneous and permanent, the inevitable and penetrating, but particularly the creative character of his religious ideas.

In *The Two Sources of Morality and Religion,* Henri Bergson singles out two qualitatively different types of morality and religion, which correspond to two types of society: a static, institutional religion for the closed society, and a dynamic one for the "open" society, the latter being in principle co-terminous with mankind. The mystics manage to pierce for a while the closedness which then closes its ranks again because religion as well as morality can be experienced only statically by the masses. This last condition arises from the very nature of men, which compels them to live in society. Occasionally the *élan vital et créateur* bursts forth in gifted individuals, who, geniuses that they are, appear extremely seldom. They arouse repercussions in the rest, but precisely because the intuitions born of their genius become common property, they shrink down to the common level of *société close*. Bergson next calls attention to two remarkable phenomena found among the *mystici:* their unstable equilibrium, which characterizes their disposition for a time, and their wonderful unerring, creative activity, which appears to be carried on without effort and is intuitively adaptable to all circumstances. Often one discovers among these "spiritual" souls an uncanny sensitivity for practical possibilities. One need but think of Teresa of Avila and her astounding monastic foundations, and of Catherine of Siena with her ecclesiastical politics.[2] Reference to the notions of the French philosopher, which exerted such great influence before the last war, does not indicate complete concurrence. To be more specific, it seems to me that his differentiation between the two classes of society, between morality and religion, is itself too "static" and too detailed. But he gives an original and serviceable analysis of the *homo religiosus* and a beautiful description of the two tendencies which are active in humanity and in society and can simultaneously appear within the same man and the same society.

Paul undoubtedly belongs to Bergson's type of brilliant mystic who is completely possessed by the numinous. In his company we find "the treasure in vessels of clay" (II Cor. 4:7), that unstable corporal-spiritual balance which so frequently accompanies mystical experience. We have already alluded to the apparitions which attended his conversion. Far more eloquent is the description given by the Apostle himself in II Cor. 12 of his revelations and visions, and of his "weakness." It is a classical text of Christian mysticism.[3] "I know a man in Christ who fourteen years ago—

---

[2] "The closed society is that whose members hold together, caring nothing for the rest of humanity, on the alert for attack or defense, bound, in fact, to a perpetual readiness for battle. . . . A force of unvarying direction, which is to the soul what the force of gravity is to the body, insures the cohesion of the group by bending all individual wills to the same end. . . . Never shall we pass from the closed society to the open society, from the city to humanity, by any mere broadening out. The two things are not of the same essence. The open society is the society which is deemed in principle to embrace all humanity" (trans. R. A. Audra and C. Brereton, Doubleday Anchor Books, Garden City, N.Y., 1956, pp. 266–267).

[3] See on this point the fine book by Anselm Stolz, *Theologie der Mystik,* Regensburg, 1936.

whether in the body I do not know, or out of the body I do not know, God knows—such a one was caught up to the third heaven. And I know such a man—whether in the body or out of the body I do not know, God knows—that he was caught up into paradise and heard secret words that man may not repeat. Of such a man I will boast; but of myself I will glory in nothing save in my infirmities. . . . And lest the greatness of the revelations should puff me up, there was given me a thorn for the flesh, a messenger of Satan, to buffet me. Concerning this I thrice besought the Lord that it might leave me. And He has said to me, 'My grace is sufficient for thee, for strength is made perfect in weakness.' "

Connected with this weakness we find in the Apostle an incredible activity, great ability to organize, good common sense, knowledge of men, and the art of "winning friends and influencing people." But primarily and pre-eminently we recognize in him, too, that brilliant intuition which was directed, not to the *société close* of Pharisaic Judaism, but to all humanity. He ascribes it to divine revelation, but the peculiar expression which he uses for it in Gal. 1:15, 16 cannot be accidental; there it says literally: "But when it pleased Him who from my mother's womb set me apart . . . to reveal His Son in me." One might describe his most personal religious intuition as the realization of *the merciful God who justifies the impious,* and the accompanying freedom of the Spirit and the primacy of love. This meant a complete break with the closed society of Judaism, but also with the provincialism of most Jewish Christians up to the moment, because it included the annulment of the Law which they (and he himself formerly) had considered the only effectual brake on sin and the basis of morality. By virtue of his ideas and of his wonderful activity, he succeeded in effectualizing the actual emancipation of the "unclean" Gentiles within the Church.

However, in the spirit of Bergson one might ask oneself whether his profound intuition, precisely because it was taken over by the community, could really be maintained in all its purity. The

Church is essentially and by intention of her Founder, the "open" society *par excellence,* destined to embrace all mankind. But she compasses her essence only imperfectly. The tragedy of her history lies in the continuing tension between her destiny of world-wide love and the tendency toward uncommunicativeness through alliance with earthly powers and desires. The care for souls as an institution is aimed at the masses and cannot dispense with a certain "static" closedness. Jesus could save the "masses" without harming the liberty of the individual. But to be active in a way which simultaneously frees from want and leaves spiritual liberty is given but to a few. It is possible only where love surpasses solicitude, and thus liberty reigns supremely in the person who cares.

The notion of God's sovereignty, which was also alive in the Old Testament and in Judaism, finds a strong and consequently original expression in the epistles of Paul: "Therefore He has mercy on whom He will, and whom He will He hardens. Thou sayest to me: Why then does He still find fault? For who resists His will? O man, who art thou to reply to God? Does the object moulded say to him who moulded it: Why hast thou made me thus?" (Rom. 9:18–20). But what characterizes his notion of God above is the combination of this thought with that of God's grace and mercy, particularly in that special manner in which he had been granted the experience of divine mercy. For the Old Covenant was not ignorant of God's omnipotence and mercy, as we have already noted in the first chapter of this book. What strikes us in the Apostle is the overpowering idea of God's supremacy and His dominating "honor" and "renown" (cf. Rom. 4:20; 16:27; I Cor. 10:31; II Cor. 1:20; 4:15; Gal. 1:5; Phil. 1:11; etc.) on the one hand, and the manner in which this sovereign God wants to actualize His universal grace on the other. Contrasted with his profound intuition of the common sinfulness and impotence, and more or less corresponding to it, is his burning sense of God's mercy for all men. He sees Jesus no longer as the Jewish Messias of Jewish eschatology, but as *Adam,* as Man (Rom. 5:14; I Cor. 15:21, 44–49), as the Head of the human race and even of the universe (Eph. 1:10; Col. 1:15–20; etc.).

His God is a God of grace and mercy for all. "They are justified freely by His grace through the redemption which is in Christ Jesus" (Rom. 3:24). "But where the offense has abounded, grace has abounded yet more; so that as sin has reigned unto death, so also grace may reign by justice unto life everlasting through Jesus Christ our Lord" (Rom. 5:20–21; cf. I Cor. 15:10; Gal. 1:15; Eph. 2:5, 7). It would appear at times that he almost delights in broadly describing the sinfulness and misery of all without exception in order to exalt God's divine mercy all the more and thus "give honor to God" alone (for this is the point where the absolute sovereignty and long-suffering mercy decisively meet in his notion of God). For this reason too, his "faith" is the highest glorification of God (Rom. 3:27; 4:20), for to believe is nothing else than to acknowledge that one owes "the grace in which he stands" (Rom. 5:2) entirely to God's graciousness.

Perhaps this great insight of the interrelationship between mercy and immeasurable glory appears nowhere more forcefully than in the passage with which Paul closes his reflections on the mystery of Israel in the central portion of his letter to the Romans. He addresses himself here to the Gentile Christians. In the preceding section he had pointed out that the temporal refusal of the majority of Jews to believe in Christ ("their disobedience") had been in God's design a means for bringing the Gospel to the Gentiles, who had previously been excluded by God and his community. But God never repents of His gifts and will one day save the Jewish people in its entirety and remove their sins. "For as you also at one time did not believe God, but now have obtained mercy by reason of their unbelief, so they too have not now believed by reason of the mercy shown you, that they too may obtain mercy. For God has shut up all in unbelief, that He may have mercy upon all." At this thought of universal grace, he bursts forth into a hymn of praise of God, such as is the ultimate purpose of both creation and redemption. "Oh, the depth of the riches of the wisdom and of the knowledge of God! How incomprehensible are His judgments and how unsearchable His ways! For who has known the mind of the Lord, or who has been His counsellor? Or who has first given to Him, that recompense should be made Him? For from Him and through Him and unto Him are all things. To Him be the glory forever, amen" (Rom. 11:30–36; see also 15:9; Eph. 1:12; 2:4; etc.).

The grace of God has in Paul's terminology primarily that original meaning of the divine graciousness and benevolence as the direct opposite of justice,[4] but including also the grace that flows from this. In current Catholic usage the term generally has the second meaning, with the result that a certain commercialization of the concept is not entirely excluded; hence there is the danger of disregarding the ever-present relationship with the personal God. Furthermore, these attributes of God, His grace, mercy and justice, must not be conceived as something static. Naturally, one may consider them as permanent qualities, but in the spirit of Paul and of the entire Scriptures we must view them primarily in connection with God's activity. God shows Himself to be gracious and merciful by His deeds. In the Bible, God is a God who acts, who reveals Himself in history, who by His *magnalia,* His wonderful deeds, enters into the world of men. The much quoted phrase of Pascal is fully in order here: Not the God of the philosophers, but of Abraham, Isaac, and Jacob. And Paul realized well that God's most glorious and decisive act was the sending of His Son and the redemption of the world through Jesus' death on the cross. "But now the justice of God has been made manifest independently of the Law, being attested by the Law and the

---

[4] *Direct opposite,* not because grace and justice exclude each other, but rather balance one another. As a Jew, Paul could not but vindicate the justice of God. He did this chiefly in two ways: first, by the traditional doctrine of God as a just judge who will reward good and punish evil; secondly, by boldly identifying grace and justice. God justifies the sinner gratuitously, which means that He mercifully grants him "justification," and by *grace* puts him in a position to achieve justification (for which the Old Law strove but could not accomplish because of the impotence of the "flesh"); see Rom. 3:21–26; 8:3–4.

Prophets; the justice of God through faith in Jesus Christ upon all who believe. For there is no distinction, as all have sinned and need the glory of God. They are justified freely by His grace through the redemption which is in Christ Jesus, whom God has set forth as a propitiation by His blood through faith" (Rom. 3:21–25).

The erection of the cross of Christ in the central point of the world's time and sin marks the revelation of God as the *merciful* judge. The *magnalia* of the Exodus, of the liberation of Israel from Egypt, all stood in relation to this great act of salvation (I Cor. 10:1–11). And Paul also understood that the grace of God has a paradoxical character: it is an act of mercy, of "weakness," and "absurdity," just as the cross, standing annoyingly there against the skyline, remains foolishness and an enigma for the powers of this world. For the folly of God is wiser than men, and the weakness of God is stronger than men (see I Cor. 1:18–31). And building on this gesture of mercy, and continuing in like vein, God continues to act by justifying sinners, by giving the Spirit of Jesus to both Jews and Gentiles, and by the coming consummation in glory. By all this God reveals Himself to the believer as the gracious, merciful and powerful God.

If we now compare Paul's sketch of God with that of the Synoptic Gospels, we note a strong similarity, not only in the over-all picture, as might be expected, but also in that which is peculiar to each of the two. It is indeed true that Jesus, even though He clearly stated the principle of universality, limited His personal mission to His own people in Palestine, but His association with that people signified a breakthrough from the closed social form and a setting aside of the moral-religious taboos. His association with sinners and publicans and His preference for the outcasts of society proclaimed God as the heavenly Father who is merciful to all. Paul preached this by word and deed with regard to the Gentiles whom the "just" Jews considered as sinners and as unclean (cf. Gal. 2:15–16). And this attitude of the Apostle was not an expression of one or other liberal breadth of spirit, or of smooth, palliative politics. On the contrary, he depicted the sinfulness of the Gentiles with all the resources of Jewish polemic, corroborated with those of his oratorical ability (Rom. 1:18–32). But to the Jew who listened with approval to this prosecution, he adds sharply: "Wherefore, thou art inexcusable, O man, whoever thou art who judgest. For wherein thou judgest another, thou dost condemn thyself. For thou who judgest does the same things thyself" (2:1 ff.). All are under sin, the Jews as well as the Gentiles (3:9); nevertheless, God is the God of the Jews, and of the Gentiles also (3:29). This was his particular "intuition"; thanks to the revelation granted him, he drew the full conclusion from the proper Jewish concept of the ONE GOD ("Hear, O Israel, your God is one God"). For this it was necessary that at the gate of Damascus there should rise for him the light of the cross and resurrection of Jesus—of the gracious and omnipotent God "who gives life to the dead and calls things that are not as though they were" (Rom. 4:17). From that moment forward he wanted to supplant the Jewish religion of justice by a religion of love, and the burden and compulsion of the Law by the morality of freedom.

Catholic spirituality has never denied these truths. It can never do so without abandoning its own character of catholicity. Perhaps one ought to say that the practical asceticism of the last centuries has laid too much emphasis on effort of will and not taken sufficient account of the central truth of the grace of God and the freedom of love. Under the influence of their crusade against Protestantism, men tended to restrict the utterances of the Apostle on the mercy of God, who justifies the impious, to the first justification, to which they certainly apply. But the Apostle teaches us most explicitly that God's merciful treatment of the impious is an example and type of all His dealing with men, and the faith of the just consists in a continued acknowledgment of this reality. *"That is the way God deals with us,"* he says and explains it in a more or less theoretical manner; but we discover it in a practical manner in Jesus' cordiality, in His sayings concerning the sick and the wealthy, the just and sinners. A system evoking commercial, quantitative and complete perfection where the emphasis is

placed, intentionally or not, on human efforts, successes and failures, disheartens the majority and puffs up that minority which
intends to succeed; and both are in conflict with the true nature
of Christianity. I do not assert that traditional asceticism must
necessarily lead to this result; who is there who will despise the
wisdom of so many centuries of Christian experience? This is
certain: only the Christian who does his utmost to live according
to God's will experiences how greatly man needs God's grace.
However, I am further convinced that at all times, and especially
in our own of spiritual collapse, Christianity must manifest itself
to the world as primarily a matter of intersubjective relationship,
as the situation of a man standing helpless before the merciful
God in the body of Christ which is the Church (and in principle
"l'humanité entière"). With Paul we must preach the cross of
Christ as the manifestation and source of God's grace. We must
proclaim the sacred contemplation of that cross, by which man is
elevated and turns his eyes away from his own misery as he reflects on Him who for us "has become God-given wisdom and
justice, and sanctification, and redemption" (I Cor. 1:30).

TEN

Flesh and Spirit

FEW PASSAGES of the Apostle have found greater response in our Western world than that of Rom. 7:7–25. In the section preceding, Paul had triumphantly described how the Christian, sharing in the redemption of Christ by faith and hope, is released from the sentence and the "wrath" of God and from the power of sin (chapters 5 and 6). In 7:1–6 he adds that the Christian is also redeemed from the bond of the Law, because he belongs "to an Other, to Him who rose from the dead." Chapter 8 culminates this grandiose vision by holding up to the Christian the prospect of heavenly glory and victory over death. Paul sees the Christian life as a liberation from the elements which we call the state of irredemption, namely, sin, the Law, the flesh, and death. Seen in this context, 7:7–25 is really a digression, an excursus on the impotence of the Law, occasioned by the contrast of Christian freedom with that of the Torah. This point, particularly, sounded utterly incredible to the ears of the Jews, especially to the pharisaic Jew. Is the Law then not in rapport with God? How can salvation and sanctification result from a loosening of this bond?

"What shall we say then? Is the Law sin? By no means! Yet I did not know sin save through the Law. For I had not known lust unless the Law had said, 'Thou shalt not lust.' But sin, having thus found an occasion, worked in me by means of the commandment all manner of lust, for without the Law sin was dead. Once upon a time I was living without law, but when the commandment came, sin revived, and I died, and the commandment that was unto life was discovered in my case to be unto death. For sin, having taken occasion from the commandment, deceived me, and through it killed me. So that the Law indeed is holy and the commandment holy and just and good.

"Did then that which is good become death to me? By no means! But sin, that it might be manifest as sin, worked death for me through that which is good in order that sin by reason of the commandment might become immeasurably sinful. For we know that the Law is spiritual but I am carnal, sold into the power of sin. For I do not understand what I do, for it is not what I wish that I do, but what I hate, that I do. But if I do what I do not wish, I admit that the Law is good. Now therefore it is no longer I who do it, but the sin that dwells in me. For I know that in me, that is, in my flesh, no good dwells, because to wish is within my power, but I do not find the strength to accomplish what is good. For I do not do the good that I wish, it is no longer I who do it, but the sin that dwells in me. Therefore, when I wish to do good I discover this law, namely, that evil is at hand for me. For I am delighted with the law of God according to the inner man, but I see another law in my members, warring against the law of my mind and making me prisoner to the law of sin that is in my members. Unhappy man that I am! Who will deliver me from the body of this death? The grace of God through Jesus Christ our Lord. Therefore I myself with my mind serve the law of God, but with my flesh the law of sin" (Rom. 7:7-25).[1]

The explanation of this passage is entirely determined by the question: What is meant by the "I" which occurs in verse 7 and will then not leave the stage till the end? One may compare this

---

[1] In the beginning of this passage Paul uses the term "commandment" as a variation for "law." One may consider this as the exact equivalent of the Torah, but there is also an allusion to the commandment that was given to Adam. Later he uses the term "law" in a more general sense, in the Greek sense of principle, orderliness. These instances are indicated in the translation by writing the word "law" with a small letter; elsewhere the "Law" means the divine Law, the Torah of the Old Testament.

section to a drama with three actors, three personifications: "I," the Law, and Sin. The first perishes miserably; or to put it better, would perish miserably if there had not been a redemption by Christ (v. 25a; 8:1 ff.). Before the sending of God's son, sin was the supreme victor (8:3). The Law, coming from God, is on the side of good, but is shamefully abused by sin in achieving its own goal, which is the death of man; in this paradox one might even see the *peripeteia* (the sudden reverse) of the tragedy, in Aristotle's sense. All this means that we are dealing here with a literary structure, and that the writer was counting on an intelligent, not a literal interpretation.

That this is not easy has been sufficiently proved by the history of the exegesis of this passage. In the Western Church St. Augustine's authority especially exerted a profound influence on this point as it did in so many others. In his later years, when the conflict against Pelagius' overestimation of nature played a prominent part in his theological thinking, he rejected the older interpretation of Rom. 7 which he himself had formerly embraced. Paul is said not to have spoken here of pre-Christian existence but, especially from verse 14 on, of his own Christian existence and of the struggle of the man who has been reborn by grace. Even the Christian, particularly the Christian, is thought to be torn asunder by the irreconcilable antagonism of flesh and spirit, of the higher and the lower element within himself. The undisputed authority of this Father of the Church was the reason that even Thomas Aquinas preferred this opinion, though the other was not unknown to him. It found a strong revival in the Augustinian renaissance from Baius to Jansenism,[2] and was adopted

---

[2] See, for example, the commentary of Estius, which for the most part is commendable. A poetic paraphrase of Rom. 7:18 ff. can be found in Racine's *Cantique Spirituel II*. Augustine's role is superbly described by Jean Guitton (*Essai sur l'amour humain*, pp. 57–58): "It is true that in the development which we have been tracing there occurred a fortuitous circumstance with far-reaching consequences to complicate the whole business; I am referring to the influence of St. Augustine, or better to the correlation which arose between the history of St. Augustine and the experience of Western man; for St. Augustine would not have been so imitated and so loved if the Latin

even earlier by the Reformers. It is still accepted by some Protestant exegetes, and even from Catholic pulpits one can often hear applications of Rom. 7 to the Christian status and struggle. This interpretation of Rom. 7 and of other texts of the Apostle (as, for instance, Gal. 5:16–26) which are incorrectly associated with it, as will appear later on, has exerted an inestimable influence beyond the pale of a properly theological sphere. We need but think a moment of the Puritanical ideas on morality, or of some modern novels, such as Julien Green's *Moira*. There are even those who think that in Paul they can detect a sort of Freudian viewpoint between the lines.

Whatever opinion a person may hold about existence and the nature of a dualism of flesh and spirit in every man, and about the general validity of Ovid's observation, *Video meliora proboque deteriora sequor,* this much is certain at least, that in the past, people were much too inclined to read their own experiences into the words of the Apostle. Puritanism is exegetically unjustifiable. Modern exegetes acknowledge in ever-increasing numbers what already the Greek and the older Latin Church Fathers had recognized in Rom. 7:7 ff., that Paul is speaking of the non-Christian man who opposes the demands of God's law. It is quite possible, though far from certain, that his own pre-Christian existence-under-the-Torah influenced his choice in the personification of the ego. But, if this is so, it must be added at once that he now judges this personal experience from the vantage point of his insight as a Christian and an apostle as constituting a type of

---

soul and flesh had not recognized its own picture in his story. With Augustine, the division between flesh and spirit has been brought to its keenest point because of his sensual temperament, by those Manichean years when he canonized nature, by his reading of Saint Paul, by the experience of an almost sudden conversion, by his opposition to Pelagius, the monk of Brittany who, imbued with optimism, certainly admitted the conflict between the flesh and the spirit, but believed that a strong will and asceticism sufficed to curb it. By force of so many concurring circumstances, to which must be added the charm of a nature enriched by love, Saint Augustine was found to diffuse a sort of luminous cloud in which the Middle Ages lived and which descended on the 16th century as a violent tempest."

the non-Christian existence in general, and hence he does not express the opinions and impressions he had before his conversion. How Saul viewed his life under the Law at an earlier period, he indicates clearly in Phil. 3:2 ff. *At that time* he did not feel a tragic struggle for an unattainable ideal, but pride and joy at the "gain" and the advantages of his legalistic justice.

It seems therefore preferable to disassociate the *ego* entirely from Paul's personality and to look upon him as the representative of every man and even of all mankind in its relationship to the law and sin.[3] That the Apostle is also mindful of the history of the human race is evident from the unmistakable allusion to the story of Gen. 2 and 3: the "commandment" refers to the prohibition imposed on Adam, which brought him and all humanity death because he did not obey (7:9–11; cf. Gen. 2:17; 3:19); the "deception" of sin reminds us of the temptation by the serpent (7:11; cf. Gen. 3:13 and II Cor. 11:3). At the same time, however, these words describe every man's growth to maturity and moral responsibility. It is only when he has come in contact with the Law by education and instruction that he can sin in fact. But at that moment he also "dies" because he is carnal and actually does transgress the commandment of God. The Jewish man is naturally first alluded to in this personification; but the Gentile is not excluded because God's law applies to him too (cf. Rom. 2:12–16). It is not without reason that the Apostle chooses from the Torah the prohibition which sounds most vague: "Thou shalt not covet." Philo, too, uses the last precept of the Decalogue to arrive at a general perspective, but according to the Stoic scheme of the passions (*De Decal.,* 142 ff.).

It is equally important to add to this description of the "I" in Rom. 7 yet another important qualification. This passage does not offer a psychological analysis, but a literary construction designed to aid the controversy. The conflict with Pharisaic Juda-

---

[3] In the Bible story the first man is represented both as a particular person and also as "man" (*ha-'adam*). In a Jewish manuscript from the end of the first century we read: "Each of us has become his own Adam" (*Syr. Apoc. Baruch,* 54, 19). It reminds a person of the character of "Everyman."

ism [4] is evident throughout. The passage sketches the human situation just as it flows from the logically thought out Jewish system. *This* man is confronted, confronts himself with the clearly recognized demands of God, which are incarnated in the commandment and in the Torah, but he *cannot* fulfill the Law, because he is only "flesh," devoid of the "spirit," which is to say, grace. The word "spirit" does not even occur in Rom. 7:7–25, but it does so in the context immediately preceding and following, where Paul speaks of the Christian situation, and in which the Pauline *pneuma* is precisely the determining factor (see 7:6 and 8:2 ff.). Basically Rom. 7:7–25, in spite of its general terminology, is directed against the Judaizers and against every religious outlook which is akin to it. Man, whether Jew or Gentile, is not outside the pale of grace, *unless he so chooses.* And it is inconceivable that Paul, who in Rom. 2 admits the real possibility that a pagan should fulfill the law of God and thus be truly justified, thanks to the prerequisite grace (2:6–29), will be able to declare a few chapters later that not a single non-Christian is capable of leading a truly moral life. The hypothesis of Rom. 7 becomes real in the system against which Paul argues, and in the existence of every man who refuses to acknowledge religious impotence, whose presumptuous autonomy bars the way to the divine help which in Christ is proffered every man. Here we have the portrait of the ambitious and the proud man, not of the poor sinner who acknowledges his faults and confesses his weakness to God. The Pharisee, not the publican of the parable, can recognize his image here, in spite of his boast of fulfilling the Law. The real purposes of the Torah, which are justice and mercy, he left unfulfilled. The still common view that Rom. 7 refers principally to the conflict between reason and the "lower" instincts reduces this powerful picture to a mere caricature. The real meaning is on a deeper level, that of religious existence in the full sense of the expression.

I have treated this passage somewhat in detail because it is

[4] Either Pharisaism proper or that closely allied early-Christian tendency which is called "Judaizing."

frequently misunderstood and because it affords an excellent starting point for discussing the notions "flesh" and "spirit," which play such prominent roles in the epistles of Paul. The contrast between the flesh and the spirit is by no means unfamiliar to the Apostle. But it is important to determine exactly the biblical and particularly the Pauline sense of these notions. Whenever we [5] speak about the body we do not think either consciously or unconsciously of the whole man, but only of a part of man, and precisely of that part of the human entity which is of "lesser worth" than the soul or spirit. With the usage of the term body there is entailed for most of us, whether implicitly or explicitly, a differentiation from the soul, even a contrast with the soul. This dualism is yet stronger in the combination "flesh and spirit"; flesh carries with it a decidedly pejorative connotation, as being the "lower" part of man, which with its lusts and instincts drags him down, and which he must know how to sublimate by gradually spiritualizing or at least controlling it.

It is precisely this usage which corresponds only partially to that of Paul, and thus becomes a source of misunderstanding of which most people are not aware. By body and flesh he does not understand exactly [6] the same as we. The reason for this can be traced on the one hand to the difference between Greek and Israelite thought, and on the other to the personal vision of the Apostle. Our terminology for body and soul, matter and spirit, and kindred concepts is largely determined by Greek philosophy. But Paul was a Jew, and even though as a Jew of the Diaspora he had already in his youth and certainly in later years after his conversion experienced the influence of Hellenic culture, his anthropological terminology (body, flesh, soul, spirit) is nonetheless originally Jewish–Old Testament, and not Greek. Traces of a

[5] "We," i.e., most contemporaries and preceding generations of the past centuries. Modern psychology, phenomenology, and existentialism hold a different view on the body and things corporal which in some points bears a remarkable resemblance to the ancient Semitic concept of self; however, this opinion is not yet generally accepted.

[6] There is naturally some overlapping.

more Greek-colored psychological terminology in his epistles are quite rare.[7] If we are to grasp his Christian and apostolic conception of the flesh and the spirit, then we must begin with the Old Testament.

In the books of the Old Covenant the term "flesh" preferably [8] signifies the whole man or the whole of humanity, in the solidarity of concrete, created existence. The biblical doctrine of man is pre-scientific, not analytic, and focused on the totality. The word "flesh" does indeed connote a contrast, but not one *within* the domain of man or the human, but man's opposition as a whole to God, of the world of the human, mortal, perishable, creaturely, to the world of God, the immortal, omnipotent Creator. A few texts from among many will quickly clarify this. In the days of Noe "all men lived corruptly on the earth" (Gen. 6:12). "My soul yearns and pines for the courts of the Lord. My heart and my flesh cry out for the living God" (soul-heart-flesh, Ps. 83:3). "Egypt is man, and not God: and their horses, flesh, and not spirit" (Isa. 31:3). "Man may be merciful to his fellow man, but the Lord's mercy reaches all flesh" (Sirach 18:11). "All flesh is grass, and all the glory thereof as the flower of the field. . . . The grass is withered, and the flower is fallen: but the word of our Lord endureth forever" (Isa. 40:6–8).

It is from this startingpoint and against this background that we must try to understand Paul's notion of the flesh. When he writes in II Cor. 7:5, "For indeed when we came to Macedonia, our flesh had no rest," he means nothing else than *we* had no

---

[7] For the concept "body" they can be found e.g. in I Cor. 12:12–27 (Rom. 12:4–5). The notion of "body" in Paul presents its own particular difficulties, because among other things the Old Testament did not have an exact equivalent for it, as distinct from the "flesh." Paul therefore occasionally uses this term in a somewhat Greek sense, and then again in a sense that is equivalent to the biblical "flesh." It is not possible here to go into full detail of Pauline anthropology; for particulars see the excellent exposition of R. Bultmann, *Theologie des Neuen Testaments*, Tuebingen, 1953, pp. 188–199.

[8] Naturally, only the main lines of the Old Testament notion can be traced here. The Book of Wisdom, which was written much later and in Greek, for example, does not really pertain here.

rest. This is evident from the manner in which he continues the verse: "We had troubles on every side, conflicts without and anxieties within." He is manifestly speaking also of "spiritual" difficulties. Rom. 6:19 reads as follows: "I speak in a human way because of the weakness of your flesh." This usage of the term is somewhat wider, but still remains within the "natural" sphere; and we could paraphrase it as: Because of your *condition humaine,* which needs descriptive images to be able to understand the Christian reality, I am using a human metaphor. And in like manner in many other places.

The distinctive originality of his concept has its root in the intimate relationship which he discerns between sin and the flesh. The starting point, however, remains always the same, so that what he says of the "flesh" is true of concrete human existence in this world, and not exclusively nor chiefly of the body and the bodily in our sense of the term, that is to say, as distinct from the immortal soul. He holds tenaciously to the Old Testament line throughout. In the light of the great revelation of Christ granted him, the Apostle also saw disclosed the most intimate nature of the human-existence-in-this-world. Christ, the new Adam, the Image of God, the real Man, is the antitype of all human being, to which in God's intention all existence is directed, and to which all responsible existence must freely direct itself if it is to achieve its proper sense and fulfillment. The "flesh," the human existence which lacks this orientation toward Christ, which is striving to self-sufficiency, is not only mortal and fickle, as the Old Testament teaches, but it is also subject to sin and the Law, and its end is death, not life. Such a man is only "carnal" and he wants to live "according to the flesh" (Rom. 7:14; 8:5, etc.). But there is always a question here of the totality of human existence which wants to be autonomous; the contrast is not between flesh and the human spirit, but between man and God, or what amounts to the same, between flesh and the Spirit of God and Christ, in whom the Christian has part by grace in baptism. For this reason both the Gentiles and Jews, so far as they refuse to believe in Christ, are "in the flesh" or "according to the flesh" (Rom. 7:5; 8:4, etc.);

flesh, in the pregnant sense of the word, determines their entire existence.

The Christian laid aside this pattern of existence when he began to believe and received baptism. It is in this sense that the Apostle writes to the Galatians: "And they who belong to Christ have crucified their flesh with its passions and desires" (5:24). Then happened what Paul calls the *crucifixion* of the flesh, because by baptism the Christian shares in a mysterious but real manner in the death of Christ, which was a death on the cross. At that time he died "to" sin (Rom. 6:11); at that moment the "old man" was crucified with Christ, and the flesh, in the meaning of existence subject to sin, was put to death (Rom. 6:6). All these expressions are basically the same.

Paul is well aware of the contrast as also of the irreconcilable conflict between flesh and spirit, but he does not completely identify this antagonism, as is evident from the foregoing, with what we generally understand by the struggle of the vital instincts against reason or the revolt of the senses against the spirit and the like. He views man as one whole, and as a whole he is "flesh" so far as he withdraws himself from the divine Spirit. What comes from God is "spirit"; what characterizes the man who arbitrarily wishes to remain by himself and to dispose autonomously of his own self and of the domain of visible nature is the flesh. That is the meaning of "living to the flesh," regardless of whether this desire for following one's own will in disobedience to the Creator expresses itself as licentiousness or as an idealistic moral-spiritual existence.

One may not therefore gratuitously interpret these sayings of the Apostle with expressions such as *le peche de la chair* of French novelists (and innumerable others), even though it is true that among the "works of the flesh" he enumerates impurity (Gal. 5:19). For he does so not because impurity takes place in the bodily or sexual sphere, but simply because it is sinful, an expression of human self-seeking, an act of wanting-to-be-oneself as opposed to God's will. For *all* sins are works of the flesh (see Gal. 5:19–21).

It is therefore characteristic of his manner of expression that he can style typically "spiritual" relationships as living or acting according to the flesh. To this belong in the first place the purely religious efforts of the Pharisees and the Judaizers who, following the conclusions of their theory, thought they could acquire holiness by their own power, independently of God's grace in Jesus Christ. This is what he writes to the Christian Galatians (3:3) who, as a result of Judaizing efforts, wanted to accept the Jewish Law as necessary for salvation: "Are you so foolish that after beginning in the Spirit, you now make a finish in the flesh?" To rely on one's own moral-religious accomplishments, he calls "relying on the flesh" (Phil. 3:3). In his view, the haughty Hellenic pursuit after "wisdom" characterizes those "wise according to the flesh" (I Cor. 1:26).

Even though the Christian has crucified the flesh and received the Spirit by faith and baptism, he still has to deal with the flesh. From the clear purport of passages such as Rom. 8:1–13 and Gal. 5:13–16, it is evident that for him it can positively become as much a menace as sin itself. Paul nowhere minutely describes the Christian's attitude toward the flesh. Using a modern expression, but one in his spirit, one might say: The Christian has conquered flesh *in principle*. It is not correct to describe Christian existence as an existence according to the flesh; but in fact a Christian can still sin and "fulfill the lusts of the flesh" (Gal. 5:16). Yet by doing so he acts contrary to his own being, which is in the Spirit and according to the Spirit. This mode of behavior, however, is present in him as a real possibility. The ecclesiastical doctrine that original sin is forgiven by baptism, but that even in the baptized person there remains a remnant of original sin, a fundamental selfishness, an evil ("concupiscence") which inclines a man toward sin, agrees completely with the sayings of the Apostle, provided only that we do not take the term "concupiscence" too narrowly. If the flesh does not characterize the Christian status, but can lead the Christian to sin, this means that it is still present in him as an

inclination to sin. In the Christian it coincides therefore with
that (radical) self-seeking against which even the man in Christ
Jesus must contend all his life.

Paul calls this struggle *mortification.* In the first section we
discussed evangelical self-denial; however, the notion of mortification in the Bible is proper to Paul. He writes to his Christians:
"But if by the spirit you put to death the deeds of the flesh,[9] you
will live" (Rom. 8:13) and: "Therefore mortify your members,[10]
which are on earth: immorality, uncleanness, lust, evil desire and
covetousness (which is a form of idol worship)" (Col. 3:5). To be
able to understand this manner of speaking, we must place it in
the larger context of life and death. Paul views Christian existence
as a sharing through God's grace in the life of Christ Himself.
It is, so to say, a gradual reflection of Jesus' own existence by virtue
of the principle of the divinely instituted solidarity between the
Master and His followers. In the teaching of the Apostle, Christ
is the new Adam, *the* Man, *the* Image of God, the Head, the First-
born. We have already mentioned this several times; but we trust
that another repetition is justifiable. This thought dominates the
entire theological thinking of Paul. In his view this existence of
Christ as Redeemer and Head of regenerated mankind is a "dying
and living." He looks upon the incarnation and the entire earthly
life as a "dying," and directed toward the end, toward the passion
and death. With the resurrection Christ inaugurates a new life,
the glorious, unimpeded life "for God" (see Rom. 6:8–10), and
this glorification includes resurrection, ascension, sitting at the
right hand of God from whence He will send the Spirit, and
the second coming. Jesus' death is in Paul's mind not only a dying "for" sin, to expiate sin, but also a dying "to" sin, to the sin

[9] Many manuscripts have "body" instead of "flesh," but there is not much
difference as far as meaning is concerned; in any case, there is question here
of flesh in the pregnant, Pauline sense of the word.
[10] A difficult expression; it is certain that here the "members" are identified
with sinful deeds, whatever they may be. Likewise the term "passion" has
in Paul a somewhat different meaning than in our usage; he can understand the term, even when standing by itself and without any other determination, as is the case here, in the sense of *evil* desires.

of mankind which He had taken on Himself "in His flesh," in His mortal existence (cf. Rom. 6:1-11; 8:2-3, etc.). By faith and baptism the Christian actually acquires a share in this "Christ-existence," in this death and life. In baptism he participates in the death of Christ, and dies to sin, the Law, and the flesh (Rom. 6:1-11; 7:4; Gal. 1:19, etc.); and begins his life for God. This is finally consummated by a Christian death and by the resurrection at the end of time. A Christian's personal, responsible life here on earth from the moment of his birth to that of his death consists in this, that, equipped with the Spirit of Christ and strengthened by the Pneuma, he "mortify," or keep "dead-like," sin to which he died in principle when he was baptized, and on the other hand that simultaneously by faith and fraternal charity he live for God. "Thus do you consider yourselves also as dead to sin, but alive to God in Christ Jesus" (Rom. 6:11). That is what it means *to be* a Christian; and that is the way he must act: "Be what you are." After this doctrinal instruction there follows the logically moral exhortation: "Therefore do not let sin reign in your mortal body so that you obey its lusts. And do not yield your members to sin as weapons of iniquity, but present yourselves to God as those who have come to life from the dead and your members as weapons of justice for God; for sin shall not have dominion over you, since you are not under the Law but under grace" (6:12-14). Pauline mortification is therefore nothing else (absolutely nothing else) than the struggle against sin as a menace to the Christian status. It is, as it were, the negative side of the Christian life which in reality cannot be separated from its positive aspect, a life for God by faith and charity, just as in baptism forgiveness of sin cannot be separated from the infusion of the Holy Spirit.

This extensive and perhaps somewhat difficult treatise of a particular section of the Apostle's doctrine, which seems to be far removed from the thinking and surely from the manner of speaking of most Catholics, simply could not be omitted. In the first place, it occupies a central point in the thought of Paul. Secondly, it can remove such misconceptions as unjustly burden him with the suspicion of fostering one or another Manichean view on life. And finally, this teaching also has great practical significance so far as it grants us, just like the evangelical logia on self-denial, a more glorious perspective of the nature and true meaning of Christian mortification.

ELEVEN

Faith Informed by Charity

WHEREAS JESUS CALLS the two commandments love for God and love for neighbor, as we have seen earlier, and Philo describes them as piety and philanthropy, for St. Paul, Christian spirituality is governed by faith in God and love for man. "For in Christ Jesus neither circumcision is of any avail, nor uncircumcision, but faith which works through charity" (Gal. 5:6).

Faith is the focal point in Paul's polemic against Judaism. Faith is contrasted with "works of the Law" or observation of the Torah (to be understood in the sense of the Pharisees), the Gospel with the Law, giving glory to God with pride in one's own achievements, and so on. This antithesis is to be found especially in the epistles to the Galatians and the Romans. We may rightfully ask if this pointed controversy which was directed at a past but concrete situation still has any meaning for us in our modern world. Would it not be much better for us to restrict ourselves to the living, contemporary voice of ecclesiastical teaching and let the dead bury their dead, all the more since proper insight into old theological distinctions can be acquired only with considerable effort? But this controversy is not ended; it must be continued at all times. As has been noted, specific Pharisaism or Judaism, or whatever name is given to that historical system which the Apostle opposed, is an essentially spiritual attitude of the religious person and, dressed with revised slogans and new shapes, belongs to our own possibilities. To discover that this polemic is meaningful to us, it will suffice to pass through the somewhat strange terminology to its basic meaning. The question here is not of rabbis and scribes of a distant past, but of the Pharisee within us and of the constant danger of self-exaltation.

The manner in which Paul handles the question is in full agreement with the abiding actuality of the real theme of the controversy. Though his language is to a certain extent necessarily determined by the jargon of a theological outlook which is no longer ours, and granting that even the great Apostle does not rise completely above the limitations of every polemic, his view on the real nature of the affair is so profound and his grasp of frequently unpleasant material is so comprehensive that his voice keeps resounding urgently and intelligibly throughout the centuries. Add to this his insistence that faith always remains the essential characteristic of the Christian posture, and as such is independent of the conflict with Judaism. This is evident from many passages in other letters; I call attention here only to the first chapter of the first epistle to the Corinthians (vv. 17–31), where the Apostle demonstrates that only faith in the Cross saves the Christian from a Greek rationalism (which for that matter merely represented universal human haughtiness in historical guise).

Between the gracious action of God, consisting in the sending of Christ and redemption through the Cross, and the sharing herein by the individual man through faith and baptism, Paul sees as a link the preaching and proclamation of the Gospel. The salvation which God achieved for man in Christ must be proclaimed and promulgated by accredited messengers. These are sent, and can rightfully speak in the name of God and the Master. Their message is called the gospel, the gospel of God, in whom everything has its beginning and to whom everything must return; or also the gospel of Christ, who sends His apostles and, so to say, is Himself the content of their proclamation. This is expressed much better in the words of the Apostle. "But all things are from God, who has reconciled us to Himself through Christ and has given to us the ministry of reconciliation. For God was truly in Christ, reconciling the world to Himself by not reckoning against men their sins and by entrusting to us the message of reconciliation. On behalf of Christ, therefore, we are acting as ambassadors, God, as it were, appearing through us. We exhort you, for Christ's sake, be reconciled to God" (II Cor. 5:18–20). "For I am not ashamed of the gospel, for it is the power of God unto salvation to everyone who believes, to Jew first and then to Greek. For in it the justice of God is revealed, from faith unto faith, as it is written, 'He who is just lives by faith' " (Rom. 1:16–17; cf. 10:4–21). Paul is the theologian of the apostolate and of the preaching of the word.[1] The message is imbued with power, the word itself possesses a divine dynamism, because God approves of it entirely, is Himself present in it. And this proclamation of grace saves man, if only it is accepted with faith.

Paul's concept of faith can in the first place be described as man's response to God's grace in Christ, which is proclaimed to him in the gospel and in the preaching of the apostles. We read the formula in its simplest form as: the Christian "believes in the gospel." From this it follows at once, as every sensible person recognizes, that this faith is not utterly irrational, but that it has an intelligible content, which must in one way or other, though never adequately, be formulated in human words and concepts. Faith is naturally not exclusively an act of the intellect, as is no fully human act, but it includes the intellect and is not achieved without reason. Paul himself in different places and in differing ways points out the object of Christian faith: "For I delivered to you first of all, what I also received, that Christ died for our sins according to the Scriptures, and that He was buried, and that He rose again the third day, according to the Scriptures, and that He appeared to Cephas, and after that to the Eleven. . . . So we preach, and so you have believed" (I Cor. 15:3–11).

---

[1] In the spirit of Paul it is necessary to distinguish between the *kerygma*, the proclamation for outsiders who are thereby enabled to arrive at (first) faith and (first) justification, and the *catechesis* for the insiders who already believe. But even this second type of faith is, in the Apostle's view, the principle of union with God and Christ; see Gal. 2:20.

The Christian believes in God who justifies the impious (Rom. 4:5), in His omnipotence which raised Jesus from the dead and shall some day cause us all to rise again (Rom. 4:24; I Thess. 4:14). In a word, he believes that JESUS IS THE LORD (Rom. 10:9). To believe, in Paul's view, means to accept one's own impotence and sinfulness [2] and to acknowledge God's omnipotence, mercy and grace. Thus it gives glory to God (Rom. 4:20—in Abraham, our prototype), and is not a "work," that is to say, not the achievement of having fulfilled the Law, thus giving man reason for satisfaction and boasting (Rom. 3:27); though it is naturally an act, even the act *par excellence,* which affects and elevates the whole man. It is the assent with one's whole heart to God's initiative, the acceptance of God's plan for salvation in Christ. While "works of the Law," regardless of their form, are the characteristic mark of religious autarchy, faith is *par excellence* the attitude of him who sees and acknowledges that he *cannot* dispose of himself in the real heart of the matter; it is the attitude of the man who entrusts all things to God.

For all these reasons Pauline faith is in the second place not only the acceptance of an intelligible proclamation and a meaningful word, it is also, and even simultaneously, the establishment of a personal relationship; it occasions an encounter. To believe that Christ died on the cross for our sins and rose as our Lord by God's omnipotence means to believe *in* God, to believe *in* Christ, to believe that God addresses *me* and will save me personally. To believe *in* someone is a biblical expression which means much more than "to accept as correct what another says." "I believe you" becomes: I believe in you, I trust you, I confide myself to you, I accept you entirely. For Paul, to believe became the essential term by which he expresses the Christian's attitude and relationship to God; to accept revelation means to accept God revealing, with all that this entails in the line of confidence, repentance, surrender and love. It seems to me, therefore, regrettable that our official

---

[2] Sinfulness and impotence in the strictest sense if there is question of the first justification, but still in a real sense even later, as has already been explained in Chapter 8.

"acts" of faith and hope do not begin with the words: My Lord and my God, I believe in You, I hope in You, as does the act of love, but with the formula: I believe that, I hope that.

We can naturally point out that our theological development of the notion of "faith" has more sharply outlined (and we might also add, impoverished) our notion of "faith" than was that of Paul, and that we restrict our personal relationship to God to the act of love. But independently of the question of whether a return to the Bible is not desirable even for theological definitions, it seems to me that surely in formulas of prayer the interpersonal relationship ought to stand in preeminence.

In any event, faith is the decisive and most distinctive note of Paul's spirituality. The person who studies his epistles for the first time may be somewhat disturbed to note that while the Apostle frequently speaks of love of neighbor and also of God's love for man, he seldom or never mentions the Christian's love for God.[3] His most intimate thoughts on man's relationship to God are expressed in a different way. But on the other hand we must add that Paul was the first to know how to express that most intimate and immediate relationship to Christ. To do this he uses the term "faith." His saying, "Christ dwells through faith in your hearts" (Eph. 3:17), holds true of all Christians. Above all we must recall here his magnificent confession: "With Christ I am nailed to the cross. It is now no longer I that live, but Christ lives in me. And the life that I now live in the flesh, I live in the faith of the Son of God, who loved me and gave Himself up for me" (Gal. 2:20; cf. Phil. 3:9).

Whereas faith in its full Pauline sense summarizes a Christian's relationship toward God, *agape,* love, is the height—and the whole—of a Christian's relationship to his fellow man. The principal, but not the only, texts on the subject are Rom. 13:8–10; Gal. 5:13; 5:22; 6:2; I Cor. 13.

[3] For the sake of the record, only twice in the traditional formulas (Rom. 8:28; I Cor. 2:9; possibly also II Thess. 3:5). The text of I Cor. 8:3 is uncertain.

First it must be noted that Paul reduces morality to charity. This is not merely a simplification; it is also a development. In the mind of the Apostle charity is the beginning and end of the moral law, and that which brings morality into direct relation to religion. He views charity as a gift of the Spirit and as a direct consequence of the Christian relationship to God. And vice versa, the Christian cannot disassociate his relationship to God from his relationships to man. This unity of personal religion and living morality is found in all parts and situations of the New Testament; it is the logical consequence of the Incarnation. St. Paul presents this great principle in an impressive manner. He first admonishes Roman Christians of their duty of justice which obliges the Christian as well as the Jew or anyone else. But he cannot leave things at this stage; the commandment of justice is absorbed into a higher complex: "Owe no man anything except to love one another; for he who loves his neighbor has fulfilled the Law. For 'thou shalt not commit adultery; thou shalt not kill; thou shalt not steal; thou shalt not covet;' and *if there is any other commandment,* it is summed up in this saying, 'Thou shalt love thy neighbor as thyself.' Love does no evil to a neighbor. Love therefore is the fulfillment of the Law" (Rom. 13:8-10). And similarly, but more briefly in the epistle to the Galatians: "For you have been called to liberty, brethren; only do not use liberty as an occasion for sensuality, but by charity to serve one another" (5:13); and "Bear one another's burdens, and so you will fulfill the law of Christ" (6:2).

This is clear: the Apostle wants to substitute charity for the Law as the norm of morality. By faith and baptism a Christian is not only liberated from the power of sin, but he is also released from the bond of the Law. We have already explained briefly in the previous chapter how in Paul's mind the Torah, though coming from God, actually became the leading instrument of sin under the Jewish system. A strange paradox, which he saw clearly and expressed tersely. Instead of being a means whereby man subjected himself to God and His intentions, it became an instrument of self-affirmation against God, of a misunderstanding

of His deepest intentions, a rejection of *His* justice as it was revealed in Christ and in the Cross. It had been regarded as the
unique and indispensable means of salvation; as such it was eliminated by Jesus' death on the cross, who took upon Himself the
curse of the Law and exhausted its power by His redeeming death
(Gal. 3:13–14; Rom. 10:4). Christ is its "end."

It is not the keeping of the Law which will save the Christian,
but "faith" in Jesus. This was evident, and was accepted by all
true Christians. But Paul goes a step further. He not only denies
the saving power of the Torah, but also rejects it as a binding
norm for a Christian. The Christian "is not under the Law" in
any way. It governs his conduct no longer. "Against such people
there is no Law" (Gal. 5:23). Then *la grande peur des bien-
pensants* (the great preoccupation of right-thinking people) begins to work. What happens to morality when the only brake
on sin has been loosened? Whoever removes the Law opens the
floodgates of licentiousness. (There are traces of this concern
and Paul's reaction in Rom. 3:8; 6:1). The courage and logic with
which the Apostle refused to re-accept the Law into Christianity,
if not as a means of salvation at least as a norm of morality, are ad-
mirable. The epistle to the Galatians is the *Magna Carta* of Christian freedom. A Christian must undoubtedly avoid sin, but not
because he is obliged by the Law. Paul deduces the norms of
Christian activity not from the Law, but from the Christian experience itself.[4]

Christians are dead to sin, and therefore it is their proper
nature not to sin, or what amounts to the same thing, not to fulfill the desires of the flesh. And they are able to do this, he asserts
in a final paradox, because what the old Law had prescribed as
an obligation, as an expression of the divine complacency, is accomplished fully only by them. The *dikaiōma*, the justice, the
holiness which is implied in the purpose of the Law, becomes real
in the lives of Christians, who are dead to the Torah and have set
aside the Law (Rom. 8:3 ff.). Because they have received from
God the Spirit of Christ as an interior principle of life and action,

4 See pages 128–130 of the previous chapter.

and only because of this, they are enabled to accept the divine will. And the first fruit of the Spirit is charity (Gal. 5:22). By this we fulfill the law of Christ (Gal. 6:2). So there still is a Law? Indeed, but not one which is a "letter" and exists only outside me, but one which is a source of life, a spontaneous "fruit" of the Spirit which has been given me. The brake on sin and licentiousness is, in the Christian's eyes, not a law of any sort, as long as we take this to mean some formal precept, but it is the love of neighbor. And this does not fence us in, but sends us off into space, to borrow the psalmist's expression. Viewed positively, Christian freedom consists in this, that by the Spirit we are enabled to love men.

It is exceedingly difficult for men, and also for the Christian, to have the courage to accept and to sustain this "simplification" and apparent facilitation of morality. Considering the concrete nature of man and society, we ought perhaps say that the Pauline idea of Christian freedom, as also the vision of the Sermon on the Mount, can become reality only when Christians live according to the highest ideals of their Christian status and self-understanding and then conclude that they shall never fully achieve it in this our earthly existence. Man longs for freedom, but he endures real freedom with difficulty, as Dostoyevsky realized so well in *The Grand Inquisitor*. This, however, does not change the fact that this idea of freedom must be present in Christianity as an ineradicable tendency. What Paul was permitted to see is an ideal which will always remain before our eyes in all its fullness, as a light that tends to draw us away from ourselves. Society cannot do without laws and customs, but Christianity must rise above these with a higher intuition and animate them with the Pauline spirit, and freedom and charity. In this divine obligation, or rather in scriptural terms, in this divine calling to an unearthly morality, which is constantly renewed in the best and most zealous children of the Church, one can see an indication that the Church is in the world but not of the world. Whenever Christians are satisfied with an earthly morality they are untrue to their vocation. But in their better moments Catholics realize that they are falling short and they go on pilgrimages to the sanctuaries of the saints where they confess and receive Holy Communion. Saints and mystics are solitaries, though perhaps less so in the Church than elsewhere.

In what Paul's *agape* really consists cannot be seen better anywhere than in his canticle on charity. We may compare this chapter (I Cor. 13) with the parable of the Good Samaritan. Charity surpasses the most exalted gifts of the Spirit (vv. 1–3); it never fails (vv. 8–13). In the central portion the Apostle describes its all-inclusiveness; it embraces all the virtues. "Charity is patient, is kind; charity does not envy, is not pretentious, is not puffed up, is not ambitious, is not self-seeking, is not provoked; thinks no evil, does not rejoice over wickedness, but rejoices with the truth; bears with all things, believes all things, hopes all things, endures all things." Thomas Aquinas expresses the same thought when in scholastic terminology he calls it "the form of all the virtues," which means that it is not only the apex and the crown, but also the beginning and essential element, if one is to speak about *Christian* virtues. Paul closes his hymn of praise with the words: "So there abide faith, hope and charity, these three: but the greatest of these is charity" (I Cor. 13:13).[5]

For the Apostle, Christian life is essentially an existence which is grounded on faith and expresses itself in charity. So far as it is an existence *in time,* it may also be described as a life *in hope.* As life in time, it is directed to the future, which is God's eternity; as life in *this* time, it is attended by vexation and oppression. Christian hope is composed of expectation and patience, of ardent desire and courageous forbearance. But the Spirit gives joy (I Thess. 1:6) because pain borne with Christ is a guaranty of coming salvation. "We ourselves, who have the first-fruits of the Spirit,—we ourselves groan within ourselves, waiting for the adoption as sons, the redemption of our body. For in hope were we saved. But hope that is seen is not hope. For how can a man

---

[5] The translation is somewhat hypothetical. Paul is citing, so it seems to me, a slogan of the Corinthian Christians, which he adapts and complements with the explicit primacy of charity. The ordinary translation suffices for our purpose.

hope for what he sees? But if we hope for what we do not see, we wait for it with patience" (Rom. 8:23–25). This whole incomparable eighth chapter of Romans is permeated with what he calls *apokaradokia,* the longing expectation of the revelation of the glory of his beloved Master, which will also be the revelation of our hidden glory, of our real life that is already with God (Col. 3:1–3).

The dynamic impulse which Jesus' preaching of God's coming sovereignty lends to the Synoptic logia is found again here in Paul's burning profession of hope and hopeful assurance: "What then shall we say to these things? If God is for us, who is against us? He who has not spared even His own Son but has delivered Him for us all, how can He fail to grant us also all things with Him? Who shall make accusation against the elect of God? It is God who justifies! Who shall condemn? It is Christ Jesus who died; yes, and rose again, He who is at the right hand of God, who also intercedes for us! Who shall separate us from the love of Christ? Shall tribulation, or distress, or persecution, or hunger, or nakedness, or danger, or the sword? . . . But in all these things we overcome because of Him who has loved us. For I am sure that neither death, nor life, nor angels, nor principalities, nor things present, nor things to come, nor powers, nor height, nor depth, nor any other creature will be able to separate us from the love of God, which is in Christ Jesus our Lord" (Rom. 8:31–39).

TWELVE

The Church

A LIVELY SENSE for the mystery of the Church characterizes St. Paul's approach to piety so greatly that it must be mentioned among the most distinctive traits of his vision. It casts his whole spirituality in a unique aura. Nor can this treatment, brief as it must be, neglect this element.

From the sketch of his spirituality which we have been drafting, St. Paul may appear to suffer from a certain individualism. In the preceding chapters we have spoken almost exclusively of the relation of the individual man to his God—of the questions of justification and a sense of sin, of faith as the personal acceptance of the Gospel and personal surrender to the Master. Only from what we have said about Paul's notion of charity can one see a social dimension in his thought—social, that is, in the sense generally attributed to the word today. Now this dimension can be fully perceived only in his idea of the Church as the community of those who believe. The *agape* itself must be primarily set in this context. The fullness of charity becomes a genuine possibility only between those "who are of the household of the faith" (Gal. 6:10), between friends of God; this is so not because Christ wills a charity necessarily exclusive and desirous of rejecting others from the common affection, but because charity is grounded in the fellowship of the Spirit and is susceptible of full realization only where there is reciprocity. The Church is the society of those who have faith in Christ and love for each other.

In our times clarity of insight into the Apostle's concept of the Church carries a value of importance and pertinence. It is possible to think of the Church primarily as an institution or primarily as the community of Christians; one ought to see her as both. Since Reformation times, Catholic doctrine has emphasized the hierarchical character of the Church, which is understandable as a reaction to the imbalance of the current Protestant doctrine. But—and this seems inevitable in the world of the human spirit— a reaction to one form of distortion engenders a new imbalance, in tendency if not in avowed purpose. To put this another way, although the official teaching of the Church and to a great extent theological discussion, too, preserved and revered both aspects, still in actual experience and practice the spiritual element nevertheless drifted away from the piety and spiritual life lived by most Catholics. It is a pleasure to see that this defensive, practical imbalance belongs again to times past, thanks especially to the liturgical and Eucharistic revival of the last decades, which the Pastors of the Church initiated and of which they still remain the leaders. For nowhere better than in the living liturgy is the true actuality of this mystery revealed: "One body and one Spirit, even as you were called in one hope of your calling; one Lord, one faith, one baptism; one God and Father of all" (Eph. 4:4-6).

Yet, despite all this, many Catholics still form a warped and disparaging notion of the Church. They feel themselves set "over against" her to a great degree, rather than incorporated into her vivifying activity. Or they regard her as a sort of organization one joins to attain a certain purpose, as a kind of necessary tool "in order to get to heaven." That the Church here and now is a beginning of heaven and a projection of the full community of the saints escapes them. They are hardly aware that God is with her and that Christ is present within her. For these and for the rest of us, meditation on what the Lord himself has revealed to us through Paul will remain a privileged way to penetrate by faith into the meaning of the mystery she is.

The Apostle views the mystery of the Church, to put it briefly and plainly, in two general ways. His first idea is the Church as the *eschatological people of God*. The origin of this concept antedates Paul; it is already in evident possession among the first Christian community in Jerusalem, and even there it is rooted in the thought of the Old Testament and later Jewish tradition. Its ultimate ground is the idea that God has chosen a people for Himself, and this idea lies at the bedrock of the entire Old Testament structure. "Think! The heavens, even the highest heavens, belong to the Lord, your God, as well as the earth and everything on it. Yet in His love for your fathers the Lord was so attached to them as to choose you, their descendants, in preference to all other peoples, as indeed He has done now" (Deut. 10:14, 15). Countless texts of similar import could be added. God liberated Israel from the bondage of Egypt, He led the people miraculously through the desert, made a covenant with them on Sinai, and gave to Israel's possession their promised land. The Israelites are a people chosen; they bear God's revelation and the promises of salvation.

The thought that a particular people as such is "chosen" is not readily compatible with modern ideas and may even seem to resemble a kind of racism. It is therefore imperative to add the following two observations. First, much of the imagery of our idea of religion is colored by certain spiritualist or idealist tendencies dating from the last century; these influences are in no way in accord with the nature of revealed religion. It is true that Christianity is a spiritual and universal religion, but it is concretized and grounded, as it were, in flesh, rooted in the human phenomenon. The summit, or, if you will, the root of this involvement with this earth is found in the Incarnation itself. Jesus was born in a particular era of our history, in an actual town called Bethlehem, as a descendant of the Israelitic nation and of the house and family of David. Simultaneously He was established in glory by God as the Head and the First-born. He is the crown and glory of that particularly beloved people, Israel, whose special calling it was, as Thomas Aquinas phrased it, to give birth in carnal descent to the Redeemer of the world. For He is a new beginning, He is the cornerstone of the universal church destined to embrace all peoples. God's limiting choice, His selection, His election from a larger whole—Abraham, Israel, David, the Remnant, Jesus—all happens with an eye toward universality, but in such a way that His world-wide plan of salvation occurs in a genuinely human fashion, and is thus concretized and realized on the small basis of one family. It is in this sense that Christianity is earthy, that is to say, incarnated; it cannot be reduced to the realm of "pure ideas" or to a system entirely spiritual and even less to a solitary encounter with God. I meet God in Christ, but in Christ I also meet humanity; not humanity as an abstract notion but as a concrete reality.

The implications of all this for Christian spirituality are evident. I need develop here only the bearing of this insight on our faith in the Church. The Church, too, is not just an idea but a human reality, called together and led to sanctity by God's grace, granted, but human nonetheless and frequently much too human. And precisely as such it can become the stumbling block, the *scandalum,* as well as the purifying test of our faith. That God freely but actually chose to join His salvific activity with our human world, and thus demand of us a faith willing to accept this corporeal reality with all its ramifications is possibly nowhere more clearly expressed than in the Apostle's teaching about his own people (Rom. 9–11). From his profound reflections I cite only these two verses spoken of the "Jews," that segment of Israel which did not believe in Christ as the Savior: "As regards the gospel they are enemies of God, for your sake; but as regards election they are beloved for the sake of their forefathers. For the gifts and the call of God are irrevocable" (11:28–29).[1]

Furthermore—and this is our second observation—the idea of an automatic election based on biological data is, already in the Old Testament, gradually transcended. We find there certain indications of a universalism, e.g., in the Book of Jonas; and above all we note its appearance in many forms in the progressive

[1] Revised Standard Version.

critique of the prophets. The preaching of most of the prophets is directed to unveil the moral-spiritual basis of the concept "people of God" and to place it constantly in fuller relief. The name "Israel" gradually becomes almost identified with "God's own, chosen people," but this also entails the people's obedience to God and faithfulness to His law. Then for the first time is there question of "Israel" in the full sense. This critique, then, distinguished between the Israelitic nation and the true Israel, the people of God, and effected eventually, under divine guidance, a time of crisis and re-appraisal for the chosen people itself. These currents culminated in Isaiah's great preaching of the Remnant (which Paul adopted—cf. Rom. 9:27; 11:5) which will remain after the catastrophe has struck the masses because of their unbelief.[2]

Various passages of the Book of Daniel speak in a similar vein—we refer particularly to the vision of the one like to the Son of Man coming on the clouds, at the head "of the saints and of the most high God," which has reference not to the whole people but to a limited, holy group (Dan. 7:18, 22, etc.).

From this exceedingly brief sketch it is apparent that from the very beginning the Old Testament understanding of the people of God stressed two essential aspects. First, that the divine election is the basis of all. This assembly resulted only through the power and the love of God. "With a strong hand" He led Israel from Egypt and brought it to the Promised Land. This people is "called," "chosen," "loved" by God; it has been gathered together by Him; it assembles as a "community" in the sanctuary, before His presence. Now this is the original, the biblical meaning of *ecclesia*. From the very outset there is no question of a community having its origin in human choice, or union, or of one based on natural or ethnic lines, even though it is in fact formed within the boundaries of a particular people.

And then there is the eschatological connotation, which gradually becomes stronger. This means that God gathers His community with an eye to the end of time when the divine promises

[2] This does not imply that the masses are destined for ruin and are simply eliminated; see what was said above concerning Romans, in chapter 11.

will be fulfilled. The possession of the land of Canaan, which was promised to Abraham and his seed, is only a first warranty, and remains precarious because of the sin of the people. Israel shall be led into captivity and shall return in part, decimated and emaciated, to an existence which is but a shadow of the glory dreamed of. And even God's judgment, which the Babylonians had executed upon Jerusalem, was not the final and decisive one. The bitter and fearful Day was still to come. When the end of time dawns, only a "remnant" will be saved. Only the "saints of the Most High" shall see salvation, those who have received the gift of the Spirit.

After Jesus' ascension, the little flock in the upper room in Jerusalem saw the Spirit descending upon them; they understood that the "final age" had come, and that these few score were the definitive "Israel," the bearers of the promise, the new beginning. They were seized by the firm conviction that they constituted the assembly of God. And this was not as in past times when a few chosen men received the Spirit for a limited time; now the whole community received the divine gift of the Spirit, an unmistakable sign that the time of decision was upon them. And Jesus, glorified at the right hand of the Father, the Lord and Messias, was the source of the Spirit poured out upon His own. Only one response was open for all those who witnessed this event: Turn your hearts and believe in Jesus! This climactic moment is the moment of grace and the moment of judgment for those who refuse belief (Acts 2; the details are given in Peter's speech). It is true to say that here the total Church was present in living reality—on the smallest possible scale, granted, but already constituted in its total essence: the Spirit of Jesus, mutual love, preaching, conversion, faith, and sacraments. Here stands the source of the Christian concept of the Church, and note that it is a concept in direct continuity with Old Testament reality. For the Church is the fulfillment of the promises; the faithful are the called, chosen, and beloved people.

St. Paul's idea of the Church is in direct relation to all of this. However, there is a particular nuance which he likes to stress in accordance with "his gospel." It was already included in that very first experience of the first Christian Pentecost, and the writer of Acts has clearly pointed it out in his account. But, from what follows in his book, it becomes evident that even the Twelve were at first not fully aware of the decisive action of the Spirit of God in his radical destruction of all lines of demarcation between peoples, in His intention that the Gentiles would become members of the Church without first acquiring membership in the Jewish nation. It remains true that the Church was grafted on the stem that was Israel and built on the faithful remnant, and that the Gentiles as such are only wild branches (Rom. 11:16 ff.); but once taken up into Christ, all are one and none are inferior to others. This incorporation into the Lord occurs through faith and baptism —independent of circumcision and the observance of the Law, which, consequently, can no longer be demanded of Greeks.[3] Even the "Gentiles" who believe in Christ are the chosen, the beloved, the saints. Paul never tires of repeating this time and time again in the introductions to his letters (Rom. 1:7; I Cor. 1:2, etc.). They are "citizens with the saints and members of God's household: built upon the foundation of the apostles and prophets with Christ Himself as the chief cornerstone" (Eph. 2:19-20).

Thus, in the spirit of the Scriptures we can describe the Church as *God's people en route,* as the community chosen by our Lord and gathered together for Him, and now on the march to the Promised Land. This idea is prominent in the Roman liturgy, where in countless places there is mentioned the *plebs tua, familia tua:* your people, your own.

What this approach to the mystery of the Church can mean for the spiritual life is plain. Full emphasis falls on God's initiative, His choice. Christians, as Christians, are *holy* through their relation to the holy God, who has set them aside by His calling and accepted them into His community. The eschatological di-

---

[3] Except for a few local and temporal restrictions which are imposed in order not to alienate the Jews too greatly (see Acts 15).

mension is of no less import: we are the people of the final era, we are called with a heavenly calling (Phil. 3:14), we hold our eyes toward the coming revelation of the "freedom of the glory of the sons of God" (Rom. 8:21). This ultimately unearthly character, this situation of pilgrimage, must prevent the Church from becoming either bourgeois or proletarian and from setting its roots too deeply in the world, its institutions and its organizations. To this temptation the Church is constantly exposed because it is composed of men living in the "flesh." Eschatology gives balance to the Incarnation by giving it relative proportions. There can be no escape into spiritualism and even less no adaptation to this eon and its methods of power and conflict of interests (Rom. 12:3; Eph. 6:11). Thus there is established a difficult but creative tension, characteristic of Christian existence, which may not be resolved by abandoning either the one or the other.

The view of the Church as the people of God, though originating from the Old Testament, is magnificently developed in the later epistles of the Apostle into a specifically Christian and possibly uniquely Pauline conception: *the Church is the body of Christ*.[4] The notion of the "people of God," deriving as it does from the Old Testament, does not indicate clearly the significance of Christ for the Church. In this second idea, however, our Lord stands totally at the center. Furthermore, the comparative particularism of the people of God and the related *de facto* selection and choice by God cede to a direct and explicit universality. The idea of the body of Christ, particularly as it is developed by Paul in the letter to the Ephesians, is all-inclusive and total.

In his teaching of the Church as the body of Christ, Paul places at the very center the relation of the community of the faithful to our Lord. Christ is Lord of the Church—this must be the first thing said. In his letters to the faithful of Colossa and Ephesus, Paul locates this sovereignty in the context of Jesus' supremacy over all creation. This Man, seated in glory, has been raised above all men and above all spiritual creatures. "God raised

4 The expression "mystical body" does not occur in the Bible.

Him from the dead and made Him sit at His right hand [5] in the heavenly places far above every rule and authority and power and dominion, and above every name that is named, not only in this age but also in that which is to come, and He has put all things under His feet" (Eph. 1:20–22).[6] "He is the image of the invisible God, the First-born of every creature. . . . All things have been created through Him and unto Him, and He is before all creatures, and in Him all things hold together" (Col. 1:15–17). And he adds immediately: "Again, He is the head of His body, the Church" (Col. 1:18; cf. Eph. 1:22–23). It is subjected to Christ; all its authority, its entire mission, all derive immediately from Him. The Church must be subject to Christ in all things (Eph. 5:24).

But for Paul, Christ is not only Lord of the Church, He is also her spouse (see Eph. 5:22–23), with whom she is intimately bound together, forming an inseparable unity like the unity of the head and members of a body. He calls her the body of the glorified Christ, "filled by Him who fills everything everywhere" (Eph. 1:23).[7] The body's growth is accomplished in Him "to the building up of itself in love" (Eph. 4:16). It is impossible to isolate Christ and His Church; whoever cuts himself off from her, cuts himself away from the Lord. This relationship is entirely unique; its only human analogue is the most intimate union known to man, marriage. "Even thus ought husbands also to love their wives as their own bodies. He who loves his own wife, loves himself.

[5] This is a metaphor borrowed from the Old Testament (see Ps. 109:1) and indicates investiture with supreme honor. The emphasis on Christ's supremacy over all spiritual powers (angelic or demoniac), which Paul makes in these two epistles, refers to certain notions which evidently threatened to find acceptance among the Christians of Asia Minor, who were beginning to regard these "spiritual" beings as superior to the Man, Jesus, even in His state of glory.

[6] Revised Standard Version. (Trans.)

[7] *The Complete Bible—an American Translation* (Chicago: University of Chicago Press, 1951). Eph. 1:23 is translated variously into English. The above translation is the more probable, and certainly suits the author's intentions best. (Trans.)

For no one ever hated his own flesh; on the contrary he nourishes and cherishes it, as Christ also does the Church, because we are members of His body, made from His flesh and from His bones" (Eph. 5:28–30). For the Christian the Church means more and must mean more than any other association or society, for she is life with God in Christ, "the universe and the calling of every believer" (H. Clérissac).

And she truly is that, a universe, an all-inclusive totality, and not a closed compartment of life. Christianity must never disintegrate into a new particularism. In the new man who is Christ there is no distinction between Gentile and Jew, between slave and free-man, or between classes of society (see Col. 3:11). Paul intends to emphasize, with his idea of the Church as the body of Christ, that in principle the Church embraces all men and so *is* the new man. In Christ, whose fullness she is, "dwells all the fullness of the Godhead" (Col. 2:9); in Christ God wishes to gather and to re-establish all things "both those in the heavens and those on the earth" (Eph. 1:10). The Church is *par excellence* the "open" society;[8] in principle her boundaries coincide with the extent of humanity. Christ has enjoined on her the task of hastening by word and by love the consummation of times and of realizing in the concrete that universality which is hers in principle. Until the time of the second coming of our Lord, it is her mission to proclaim salvation to all and to establish the communion of *agape* on earth. In this unity of faith and love the shepherds of the Church must be the leaders. Here, too, is the proper place of the two great sacraments Paul names, baptism and the Eucharist.[9] By baptism a person is incorporated into the community of Christ and also in consequence into the community of the people of God; and the unity in love, which *is* the Church, finds its highest realization in the meal of the Eucharistic sacrifice. "Because the bread is one,

[8] Naturally this does not exclude the idea that the normal means of salvation consists in membership in the Catholic Church as the Church of Christ; but this is not the sole way of God's grace (although she is its sole direction).

[9] See Rom. 6; Col. 2:11 ff.; I Cor. 10:14–21; 17–34.

we though many, are one body" (I Cor. 10:17), and, "As often as you shall eat this bread and drink the cup, you proclaim the death of the Lord, until He comes" (I Cor. 11:27).

Christian solidarity, as it exists in the sacred expanse of the Church, is stronger than any other, whether of family, country, personal interests, or culture. This solidarity was the miracle that led pagan antiquity to exclaim: "See, how they love one another." The greatest social differentiation of all times, the distinction between freemen and slaves, Christianity transcended (not abolished—that took centuries). The slave sat next to his master at the same Eucharistic banquet and died with him in the same arena for the sake of the same faith. "For all you who have been baptized into Christ, have put on Christ," Paul writes to the Galatians. "There is neither Jew nor Greek; there is neither slave nor freeman; there is neither male nor female. For you are all one in Christ Jesus" (3:27–28). "Bear one another's burdens, and so you will fulfill the law of Christ" (Gal. 6:2). The law is, at bottom, but one, as we have explained: love of neighbor, and this can be defined as a love which knows no human distinctions in order to accept the burdens of all humanity. Possessions divide men— whether it is to own them, to be concerned about them, or to desire to accumulate them. What unites men is being, real being, which means freedom and love; not a love of noble intentions but one which accepts and re-establishes concrete social realities, one which "bears one another's burdens."

It has become accepted in the Western world, at least among the majority, to hold forth on the subject of Communism, considering the adherents of this system as the only ones, or at least as the principal ones, guilty of the calamities which plague or threaten our system. In this context, we must not forget that as an ideal Communism is the fruit of a deep insight which might be described as the projection of a secularized mystical body. Without doubt we justly condemn the atheism and materialism which are historically bound up with the system. But we, Christians, can reject the positive tendencies of the doctrine only after we have condemned ourselves—after we recognize that Marxism first became possible only through the grave sin of Christians, the exploitation of man by his fellow man in the capitalist system, which arose in countries calling themselves Christian; after we understand that Marxism remains a real possibility only because of this, and is, consequently, felt as a threat by many only because we Christians still sin and do not sufficiently incarnate the divine plan of the mystical body. To put all this another way, because the proletarian solidarity is still at least equally strong as Christian solidarity, if not in word then certainly in concrete social reality.

We have no right to excuse our sins and negligence by an appeal to the perfection of Christian theory. The most perfect principles must yet be made real in our human world. "By this shall all men know that you are My disciples, if you have love for one another," Jesus said; and not by the fact that you possess a doctrine of love put into practice only too imperfectly. Our Lord became man and shared our human condition of suffering and death before He proclaimed his doctrine of love of neighbor. And surely it cannot be denied that the *agape* has become reality in the Church and has gloriously made itself manifest in all centuries by the self-sacrificing social love of numberless Christians. However, through the fault of many belonging to one or another professedly Christian nation, it has been realized so defectively that those outside cannot recognize it in public and social life.

Marx began from the social system in which man was exploited by man; his ideal was a world in which, according to his words, "a man should have supreme worth in the eyes of his fellow man," a world which precludes the possibility of exploitation, war, or any form of slavery. He based his struggle for this world on an informed proletariat, on the class which he considered as the universally human "class," and therefore as the universal man, the courier of the true, new humanity. He based his opinion on the fact that the proletarian was the man without possession, without land or country, without any privileges, just simply *man*—delivered up to the powers which lorded over him. The inevitable revolution must needs be violent, but Communist violence was intended to end all violence, and all compulsion, and terror.

We may naturally ask whether this ideal must not necessarily remain a mere Utopia as long as it is without God's grace; and there is hardly any need to question whether in the concrete realization of people's democracies, Communist violence has not become an institution, a tool of the party's power, and a bludgeon of the universal class. But nonetheless the ideal of a universal humanity in which nobody is exploited by another and a "man has supreme worth in the eyes of his fellow man" is at root an ideal properly Christian, which can be realized only in the mystical body. Even the expression, "man having supreme worth in the eyes of his fellow man," no matter how atheistic it sounds, admits of a specifically Christian interpretation. God became man; Christ the Man is the universal man. "As long as you did it for one of these, the least of My brethren, you did it for Me" (Matt. 25:40). Unconsciously, Communism intends to be a profane Christianity. And it became possible because in the Christian world distorted distinctions of class and property were stronger than authentic human and Christian solidarity.

The Christian believes that the perfect society is not of this world. Now this does not imply that he may *therefore* in the last analysis remain indifferent to the fate of this world. God wills the blessed, heavenly society to be dependent on the "increase of the body in love" on this earth. This occurs only under the force of the Spirit; but this becomes effective only by our participation in the proclaiming of the Word and in the exercise of charity. Christian love is a concrete love, a love creative of social reality and not active only in the purely individual sphere. It is always the essential life-function of the body of Christ, which stands open to all mankind. This, together with the perspective of final fulfillment through the second coming and resurrection, is the ultimate consequence of Paul's great vision: universal sinfulness which God's grace turns to universal salvation through belief in Jesus and love for man.

PART THREE

The
Gospel of
St. John

THIRTEEN

Godliness

By "spirituality" we have consistently understood a specific spiritual posture and *élan vital,* from which undoubtedly all sorts of practical attitudes and consequences follow, but which nonetheless primarily signifies a structuring and directing of the *spirit.* Never is this word in a more congenial context than in an effort at sketching the piety of the last Gospel, no matter how briefly; for the fourth Gospel is distinctively unworldly, limitless and "spiritual." The same may be asserted correctly concerning the spirituality of the other Gospels and of the entire New Testament, but the conviction that religion is basically a matter of the spirit and of interior posture is nowhere expressed more clearly than in the Gospel which already in early Christianity was called "pneumatic" or "spiritual."

From the earliest ages there has always been the feeling that the Gospel of John has a unique character, which distinguishes it not only from the older Gospels but also from the epistles of Paul. In the New Testament, it occupies a place totally its own. Only the letters which bear John's name breathe a similar atmosphere. When we ask, however, in what precisely this Johannine spiritual climate consists, the answer is not easily come by unless a person is satisfied with poetic classifications, and is prepared to speak with Dostoyevsky of "the white Christianity of John." Actually, very different solutions have been suggested from even the earliest periods. The Gnostics of antiquity felt at home in this Gospel, or at any event had immediate recourse to it, seeing there an opportunity to impose their own interpretation. Fathers of the Church such as Augustine pointed emphatically to its symbolism. Long before the advent of modern criticism it was recognized that its theology was as important as its history. In our day some seek the explanation of the properly Johannine element in its affinity to what they call the superior religion of Hellenism or to Gnosticism; others point to its Jewish-Hebraic character, to its strongly cultic or sacramental fabric, or to its Old Testament and primitive Christian background. The amazing thing is that not only do all these theories contain at least an element of truth (as happens in most instances), but that the first and the last impression which the reader of the fourth Gospel carries away with him is one of an outstandingly strong spiritual unity and of great consequences issuing from the viewpoint it proclaims. The writer succeeded in completely absorbing the influences which he had himself experienced piecemeal, in uniting his material into a closely-knit structure, and in creating a work which leaves an incomparable impression of unity of spirit, language and atmosphere. It is marked not only by its own character, but by the possession of its own spiritual personality.

This originality, which is so difficult to define but so easy to perceive, is also to be found in Johannine spirituality. What strikes us first is its *unworldly character*. We may recall here the well-known admonition of I John 2:15-17: "Do not love the world, or the things that are in the world . . . because all that is in the world is the lust of the flesh, and the lust of the eyes, and the pride of life; which is not from the Father, but from the world." But what is meant here is much more than merely an admonition to flee from the wicked world.

If we may summarize the Sermon on the Mount as the program of the Synoptic way of life, we see there an exalted ideal which seems hardly capable of full achievement, but we can still recognize in it some consideration for human relationships and human society. There are instructions for marriage, for association with those who are not disciples or even enemies or persecutors, instructions concerning oaths and the use of money and property, and even regarding certain practices of piety. Of all this there is no trace in the Gospel of John. Society and the world—understanding this term in our sense—leave him apparently indifferent. There is not a single pronouncement on detachment from riches or on the giving of alms, about which the Synoptic Gospels have preserved so many logia. There is nothing which may be compared to the sentence: "Give to Caesar the things that are Caesar's." In John, Jesus says to Pilate: "Thou wouldst have no power at all over Me were it not given thee from above" (19:11). Looking at the matter superficially, it would seem that we have here the same thought as Paul's "There exists no authority but from God" (Rom. 13:1). But this is only apparently so. Rom. 13:1 is a positive evaluation of earthly authority, whereas Jesus' saying in John means only that no earthly tribunal has proper jurisdiction over Him who was sent "from above."

In the fourth Gospel there is no moral teaching. There is naturally no system of ethics anywhere in the New Testament, but the basis is there, and there are rules of behavior which were susceptible of further development and application. In Paul we even come across initial indications of family and social morals (see I Thess. 4:11–12; II Thess. 3:6–13; Col. 3:18–4:1; Eph. 5:22–6:9; I Pet. 2:18–3:7, etc.). In the fourth Gospel there is only one commandment to regulate human relationships—love; and *agape* is mentioned only so far as this exists between brothers and sisters in Christ, as will be explained in due time. All this does not mean that John wants to reject traditional morality, as some Gnostics maintained. Traces of ethical evaluation can be found in 3:20–21, and in the first epistle: "My dear children, these things I write to you in order that you may not sin" (2:1; cf. 3:4; 5:17). But these are vague and general indications, and it can hardly be asserted that the attention of the evangelist is fixed on these matters. He does not seem to be concerned with those things which preoccupy the majority of people—cares, worries, money, and earthly position. In this sense he is truly "unworldly."

But then, what does he mean by the *world?* He uses this term very often, and its usage is extremely typical of his whole bent of mind. But what he denotes by it is only partially synonymous with our customary moral terminology when we speak of worldly people and of the dangers of the wicked world, and so on. In John these things lie on a deeper level; they stand in wider scope. The Greek spirit, not only in the so-called classical period but also at the height of the Stoa until far into the Christian era, did not regard *kosmos* as the neutral and unqualified "world" of the universe, but simultaneously as order, regularity, a harmonious whole, the totality of being, actually divinity itself, as manifest to the human reason, as something which encompasses and embraces man in an accommodating and dignified manner. For the perspective of the Old Testament and thus also for the upright Jew it is sufficient to cite the very first sentence of the Bible: "In the beginning God created heaven and earth." The world is created by God; it is therefore completely subject to Him, and proclaims the glory of its Creator. "The heavens proclaim the glory of the Lord." The transcendent God of the Bible can in no way be identified with the world; but neither is there any trace of an irreconcilable opposition, of an unalterable antagonism between God and the world. According to the Scriptures one could never say without qualification that God is good and the world bad. The Old Testament does not suffer from a guileless optimism; it fully acknowledges the existence of evil, of sin and suffering, but it does not personify evil, it does not make it independent from the one Creator. In one or another way, indeed in a way which astounds us and which we are bound to interpret philosophically, it brings even evil into direct relationship with God. For the Lord is good and merciful, but He is also just and omnipotent; in a word, He is THE LORD, and nothing happens independent of His will.[1] "I am the Lord, and there is none else: I form the light,

[1] Or permission, we add quickly. But the Scriptures do not distinguish explicitly between willing and permitting, between direct or indirect causality. Christian theology has been operating on the basis of the data of revelation (Scripture and Tradition) with the aid of Greek methods

and create darkness, I make peace, and create evil. I, the Lord, am the one that does all these things" (Isa. 45:7). "Shall there be evil in a city, which the Lord hath not done?" (Amos 3:6).

Much could be said about these and various other texts, but they all show without ambiguity that the perspective of the Old Testament on the world was unified and consistent. The Jewish concept was so sublime because it totally accepted this world, which it saw realistically both with its miseries and its pleasures, and placed it before the face of the one God as "the work of His hands." The Greek spirit, which could view evil only as a deviation, irreconcilable with metaphysical "goodness," really did not know what to do with it. Consequently, evil had no place in the Greek world-picture except as an anomaly to be overcome and transcended at all costs. For the Greek, the world meant correct order, uniformity, and beauty. Even in biblical thought, evil remains a puzzle; but the Scriptures do not shy away from the paradox which does not isolate evil from the all-good God. The origin of evil is not somewhere beyond the reach of the Creator. The mystery of evil is not eliminated, any more than it is separated, from the proper mystery of faith—God, who has disclosed Himself to us. This does not solve the problem but it does place it in the context of revelation, thus making it possible to accept by faith an incomprehensible mystery.

In its effort to solve the mystery of evil, the human mind came upon yet another solution, which when followed to its final conclusion leads to radical *Gnosticism*. If one abstracts from all sorts of small differentiations in its manifold manifestations, one may equate Gnosticism with the mentality which, though having its origin in the East, spread quickly in the period contemporaneous

and concepts. But this does not mean that theology is a sort of synthesis between the Bible and Greek thought. In the present instance, for example, Catholic theology continues to consider the mystery of evil, as does the Bible, in the light of the one, totally dominating mystery of the self-revealing God who created all things and guides and governs the world in its entirety. It does not destroy, so to say, the contact between God and evil, as Greek philosophy, certainly in its leading tendencies, was compelled to do.

with John and exercised great influence on the religious thought of many. At the same time it must be affirmed anew, as was done earlier for Pharisaism, that it expressed an existentialist posture, a certain way of looking at life and the world, which is part of common human possibility and is thus not limited to any particular historical era. As a matter of fact, it recurs regularly, whether in the form of different religious sects, such as the Manicheans and the Catharists, or in individual religious experience. In its more radical form it is characterized by a dualism which accepts two principles entirely independent and opposed to each other, good and evil, from which all beings have their origin with their unalterable character or "nature." Evil is thus personified; not merely separated from the "good" God, but made equal with Him, either entirely or at least as being of equal birth, and set up against Him as an autonomous fountainhead of the hierarchy of evil. A whole system of irreconcilable opposites is then constructed on this division; light is put into oppositon to darkness, spirit to matter, God to the world.

Gnosticism does not ignore in any respect these concepts so dear to the Greek; quite to the contrary, these notions are equally important to the Gnostic, but with an entirely different emotional value. Precisely because of its regularity, the cosmos now becomes the sum of evil; the compelling force of matter and bondage; blind fate, to which the chosen, Gnostic man is subjected because of his body, but from which he can escape with his divine quiddity. "The world is the plenitude of evil" (*Corpus Hermeticum*, VI, 4). For Gnosticism redemption therefore consists in overcoming the deceitful appearance of all matter, in freeing the spark of light from the darkness of the body; in ascending from this world to the realm of light; and *gnosis*—a religious "knowledge" of the true self, its origin and destination—is the only means for accomplishing this.

If now we return to the fourth Gospel and the epistles of John in order to investigate the meaning and role of the concept "world," we must first observe that here the term occurs very frequently and apparently plays a more important role than in the rest of the New Testament. At the same time we discover, and this is a matter of even greater importance, that we can no longer be satisfied with the simple and evident meaning which the notion of world has in the Old Testament and to a large extent also in the Synoptic Gospels. No less than ten times in John do we meet the expression "this world." This is a point of great significance, for it always suggests the existence of another world, which is the true world, that of God and of the divine reality. "World" is therefore synonymous with "the lower things," the realm here below. The Redeemer who brings revelation has His origin in a realm "above" (8:23). In innumerable places we read that He "comes into the world," that "He was sent into the world," and that He leaves it by "passing out" of it. Passing out of the world is synonymous with going to the Father (13:1, etc.). The disciples, likewise, do not belong to the world, but have been taken out of it. Perhaps this is stated more impressively nowhere than in those extremely simple sentences of the highpriestly prayer: "And I am no longer in the world, but these are in the world, and I am coming to Thee, Holy Father. . . . But now I am coming to Thee; and these things I speak in the world. . . . I have given them Thy word: and the world has hated them, because they are not of the world, even as I am not of the world. I do not pray that Thou take them out of the world, but that Thou keep them from evil. They are not of the world, even as I am not of the world" (17:11–16).

This cosmos is therefore an expanse, the all-inclusive place of men and their behavior and the stage for the drama of the redemption. But it is also humanity itself; humanity which does not yet believe, which must be saved, which still can be saved. "For God so loved the world that He gave His only-begotten Son. . . . For God did not send His Son into the world in order to judge the world, but that the world might be saved through Him" (3:16 ff.). But generally the term signifies that sector of humanity which refuses to believe and rejects revelation. This world cannot receive the Comforter (14:17). Those who believe do not belong to this world but are necessarily hated by it (15:18;

17:14; I John 3:1). The world does not "understand" them. Between this world and God there is an irreconcilable opposition. Christ does not pray for it (17:9). It is anti-God and anti-Christ. "All that is in the world, is not from the Father" (I John 2:16). Christ "overcame" the world (16:33); the believer is also victorious over it by his faith, by his supernatural knowledge (I John 5:4). It is subject to a master, "the ruler of this world" (12:31; 14:30; 16:11). It "is wholly in the power of the evil one" (I John 5:19). It is also a spiritual realm, an impersonal source of unbelief. They who reject revelation are "of the world and speak of the world" (8:23; I John 4:5). Just as the Lord knows His own, it also has "what is its own" (15:19).

As we examine this whole picture it would seem that the dualism is perfect and we ask ourselves wherein lies the difference between the Johannine view of the world and that of Gnosis. Is not the evil one, who was a murderer from the beginning and the father of lies (8:44; I John 2:13–14; 3:8–12, etc.) equipped with all the paraphernalia of the wicked Demiurge? There are, however, a number of texts which we have not yet cited which will, as if at the last moment, save John's view from being Gnostic. He says expressly that the world was created by the Logos, that is, by Jesus Christ (1:3, 10; cf. 17:24). He also says that God loved the world (3:16; I John 4:7 ff.); the unknown God of Gnosticism cannot love it. And finally, the evangelist leaves open the possibility that the world will do penance and have its sins forgiven (1:29; 14:31; 17:21; I John 2:2; 4:14), whereas the Gnostic world, because of its eternally immutable character, cannot do penance nor have its sins forgiven.

From this it follows that we may not interpret in a Gnostic sense his many statements on the world, no matter how dualistic they may seem. That the whole world is subject to the evil one does not mean that it was not created by God, nor that unbelievers are inevitably surrendered to the power of the devil. But it does mean that the cosmos of John is a "world" of tensions with a wide range of implications which are barely compatible with each other, extending from an almost completely neutral concept of the world to one which signifies mankind persistent and rigid in unbelief. And it is precisely this last, extremely pregnant, sense of the word which preserves it from dualism properly so-called. For the world in this sense means mankind, standing alone by its own choice because of its refusal to believe in Jesus; it does not mean human nature. In spite of appearances to the contrary resulting from his way of speaking, the universe of John is not static, it has not been previously determined and arranged according to unchangeable categories of good and evil; it is in motion, revolving about the only possible central point, which is Christ, and it is (let me repeat again) personal relationship to the Lord which determines this position. "He who believes in the Son has everlasting life; he who is unbelieving toward the Son shall not see life, but the wrath of God rests upon him" (3:36). Only those who refuse to believe in Christ and hate their brothers as did Cain are children of the devil (8:44; I John 3:8); by their deeds they manifest their own character, but their deeds are the consequence of their own choice. But the ruler of this world remains subjected to the power of the humble Redeemer.[2]

The question remains: Why does the evangelist express himself in this manner, why is his "world-view" drawn in colors that are so much darker than those of the other Scriptures,[3] and why do they show such a striking resemblance to Gnosticism, notwithstanding their basic differences? The answer can only be that the spiritual movement which we call Gnosticism was a part of the times and did not leave him unaffected. It seems quite probable that his ultimate purpose in writing the Gospel—the same applies to the longer epistle, for that matter—was not merely to make a Christian appeal to the followers of this religion which toward the end of the first century was exerting a strong and widelyspread influence as an amenable spiritual atmosphere rather than

---

[2] To understand the character of the evangelist we should note that in his Gospel Satan plays an important role as a spiritual power, but he makes no mention of the many exorcisms which we read of in the Synoptics.
[3] With the exception of a few later Pauline texts which tend in the same direction (Eph. 2:2; 6:12; Col. 2:8, 20).

a uniform doctrine; he wants to convert and correct at the same time, and to show that the Gnostic world-view can acquire real meaning only if it is centered on the incarnate Logos, and thus becomes essentially changed.

Some time ago Romano Guardini, in a very fine little book,[4] presented the hypothesis that by nature the evangelist himself tended to a dualistic outlook and had an inclination, as it were, toward a sort of Gnostic psychology, traces of which can still be detected in his writings, such as absolutism, preference for stark contrasts, keen attention to the essence and origin of things. But he overcame this dangerous inclination through his encounter with Jesus; in place of the irreconcilable conflict of essences, there came the unifying relationship to this unique, personal center. Guardini also fosters the opinion that in the striking emphasis on fraternal charity in the Johannine writings we can discern an indication that love for an individual concrete person was not particularly attractive to his natural disposition. Whatever the case may be, it is certain that he had an inner affinity to Gnosticism and that his peculiar outlook on the world is not the result of his apostolic interests alone. The manner in which he evaluates the world is so vigorous and consistent that it reveals a personal concept of the term, an idea of the world that is directly opposed to the original Greek notion, which, without being in conflict with the Old Testament or primitive Christian apprehension of the world as a creature of God, can nonetheless not be entirely explained in its specific connotations by derivation from the latter.

We have given more consideration than usual to this one important image because it was necessary to clarify in a singular particular detail what is involved also in many others: the very special nature of Johannine thought and the resultant unique character of his spirituality. Furthermore, the cohesion between the various ideas in the fourth Gospel is so strong that whenever one goes a little more deeply into one he always faces the whole. It is impossible to treat his great ideas individually and successively.

[4] *Das Christusbild der johanneischen Schriften*, Wuerzburg, 1940.

Every effort to bring a certain portion into the light necessarily directs our attention to the whole. What we called the unearthly character of Johannine spirituality may also be pointed out as its peculiar nature. It is absolute, seldom shaded; it is compressed into a few fundamental realities. It is consequently also universal, precisely so far as it is not enclosed by concrete, accidental circumstances, but takes place entirely on an existential level.

Naturally, the Gospel is not independent of the historical situation of Jesus' life; but the evangelist is constantly anxious to have the timeless element shine through the historical, and to show in the concrete relationships of Jesus to the Jews and to the disciples the essential relevance of revelation to the world and to the faithful. The Samaritan woman and the crowds of Galilee illustrate the tendency of the masses toward materialism (4:15; 6:26–29). In Nicodemus we see the hesitation and doubt of the well-intentioned intellectual. The "Jews"[5] especially, are a type of human pride and spiritual self-sufficiency, the representatives *par excellence* of the world which rejects revelation and is worthy of condemnation.

In the second part of the Gospel (chapters 13–17), it is true, the disciples find themselves in the historical situation of the final gathering and the approaching farewell, but at the same time they clearly represent the Church after Jesus' glorification. They are representatives of all believers who have never seen Christ. "If you love Me, keep My commandments" (14:15). And what are these commandments? Faith in Jesus and fraternal charity! In other words, both the disciple at the farewell and the Christian standing without Jesus in the world, who ask, "How can I still love You?," are directed to keep the commandment. Intimacy with Jesus is realized in this world by fraternal charity, and this is "earthly" only so far as it expresses itself in a willingness to

[5] In the fourth Gospel the Jews must not be simply identified with the Jewish people; "historically" speaking they are the spiritual leaders who reject Jesus; "typically" speaking they represent the "world" because they, even while appealing to the Scriptures, oppose themselves to the revelation which has come in Jesus.

help, in the form of genuine solicitude and the gift of earthly life; for, by origin it too is from above. These chapters tell us that a purely human relationship of love toward Jesus is no longer possible. They declare moreover that this has never been the case. The sentiments which the Twelve experienced before the departure of the Master was not true love. The farewell, the departure—that is, the glorification of Jesus—and the sending of the Spirit first made true love possible. But in its realization in this world, this consists in fraternal charity, and in faith as an immediate and personal relationship to the Lord. And yet faith is directed to the absent and glorified One who has no need of our solicitous love. "Blessed are they who have not seen, and yet have believed."

The piety of the fourth Gospel, in its fullest dimension, is Christocentric. "These things are written that you may believe that Jesus is the Christ, the Son of God, and that believing you may have life in His name" (20:31). His spirituality, if we may use that term yet once more, has been reduced to this one absolute and is therefore identical with Christian existence itself. It is above all a devout contemplation, a belief, an acknowledgment that Jesus is who He is: the one, the way, the truth and the life. Whoever knows Him, knows God, because He is the perfect revelation of the Father. "This is eternal life, that they may know Thee, the only true God, and Him whom Thou hast sent, Jesus Christ" (17:3). For John, "life" consists in knowing—in a positive, supernatural, divinely given knowledge, which is really a *gnosis,* a knowledge of God, an awareness of the invisible and eternal Father through the Logos of His Son. "Whoever has the Son, has life"; and one "has the Son" by believing in the testimony which the Father has given concerning Him (I John 5:11, 12). This knowledge and acknowledgment of Christ as the light, as the bread of life, as the vine, and the shepherd, that is to say, as the unique and perfect salvation of man, necessarily includes the acknowledgment that man of himself is powerless and that his gods are nothing. "Without Me you can do nothing" (15:5). This constitutes Johannine self-denial; it is entirely on a spiritual level.

It is this constant relationship to Christ in whom we have been given the fullness of life and salvation, which preserves the fourth Gospel from the pessimism of the Gnostic concept of the world. Just as Paul overcame Pharisaism as an existential possibility, not only by vehemently contradicting it but by positively transcending it with the doctrine of justification through faith, so John gives the Christian answer to the "Gnostic" question which belongs to the perennial human problems: there is an unbridgeable chasm between good and evil; a complete separation of spirits is possible. But the demarcation which sets off these worlds irrevocably is established only by every man's personal decision, by his choice of either giving or refusing faith. Faith in the Logos who became *flesh* directs man's attention to the material world, which through the Incarnation is filled with God's own glory.

FOURTEEN

Sacramental Symbols

HERE WE FACE what is indeed a paradox: the most spiritual and unworldly Gospel presses the whole material creation into its service. Matter is not only accepted; it is elevated and illumined with a divine light. John draws all his conclusions from the incarnation of our Lord, which he dramatically terms "becoming flesh." We may grant that the famous prologue, with its formulae on the Logos, on light and life, is intended to meet the spiritual aspirations of the period. An English exegete [1] has brilliantly demonstrated this with quotations from Philo, the Hermetic writings, and other representatives of contemporary Hellenistic religions. Yet this applies only to a certain extent, or more exactly, to verse 14: "And the Word was made flesh and dwelt among us." This was a slap in the face of Gnosis and of every "higher" religion. This compelled every well-intentioned reader to make his decision right from the very first page.

That all things came into being through the Logos, that in Him was light and life, and that darkness stood in opposition to Him; with all this a person could cope, and it might even appear vaguely familiar to the Hellenist. But that the divine Word had become flesh was as great a scandal to this type of reader, as was

[1] C. H. Dodd, *The Interpretation of the Fourth Gospel,* Cambridge, 1953; some of the ideas in this chapter have been borrowed from this notable work.

to the Jew the notion that this man should be God. This sort of situation is frequent in John. If in the first portion of the discourse between Jesus and Nicodemus (3:1–13) we were to omit a single word, it would almost seem that we were dealing with a philosophical dialogue on the supremacy of the spirit to matter and the necessity of a purely spiritual rebirth for every man. But that one word "water" (v. 5) is the tenuous yet firm thread which unites the whole episode with the Christian economy of matter sanctified by the Spirit of God. In 6:63 we read: "It is the spirit that gives life; the flesh profits nothing." Here you might think that the evangelist is again deprecating the material. But we must remember that he, no less than Paul, is fond of expressing his thoughts in antitheses. He wants to say that matter, when not viewed in relationship to Christ and informed by His Spirit, is dead and useless.

The whole material world points to Christ as its proper meaning and fulfillment. This spiritual realism, and this unparalleled historicity, is generally called the *symbolism* of the fourth Gospel. However, we misinterpret this term if we think only of mere metaphors without material or historical reality. The mystery of the Incarnation, of which this "symbolism" is a direct result, consists precisely herein, that in Jesus Christ divinity and humanity, both intact and undiminished, form a real and living unity. In the fourth Gospel there is a very special relationship between narration and signification, between history and theology. This relation is not established by falsifying the facts to make them serve a purpose, and even less is the significance of events grafted to the account as a sort of commentary. The facts recalled re-present a deeper meaning, which is in turn contained in the reality of the events. One might call this a realistic symbolism, which has been compared by Lagrange to the manner in which Dante portrays the figure of Beatrice, if one were to grant that she was a real, existing person. John's method holds a middle course between the purely concrete symbolic activities of the Old Testament prophets —for example, Ezechiel's drawing of the siege of Jerusalem— and the abstract symbolism of Philo, for whom persons and events

of the Old Testament were real figures—in our sense of the term
—of universal truths and processes of the soul.

The symbolism of the fourth Gospel thus understood is constructed in two ways. The first consists in styling miracles as
signs. This term, which also occurs elsewhere in the New Testament to signify miracles, has not lost its original connotation in
John. For him the great works of Jesus were not only prodigies
—astonishing, inconceivable spectacles which leave the witness
breathless; they have a meaning. To the believer they signify and
represent something which surpasses the merely wonderful and
astounding. In two passages of the Gospel there is a rebuke of
the mentality which sees only the sensational in a miracle. "Unless you see signs and wonders, you do not believe" (4:48). And
to the crowd which follows Jesus curiously after the multiplication
of the loaves, he says: "You seek Me, not because you have seen
signs, but because you have eaten of the loaves and have been
filled" (6:26). Johannine faith is not based on a miracle as a *show*
but as a *sign*. The wonderful deed points to the doer; it shows
Jesus, not only in the general sense—such as we have also in the
Synoptics—of manifesting God's omnipotence, but proves that He
was really sent by God.

The wonders of the fourth Gospel are symbols in a concrete
sense, signs of what Jesus means to the world as "Savior." They
signify through the reality of the material world what Jesus is in
the spiritual realm. Occasionally this sense is expressly indicated
by the evangelist. The gift of light to the eyes of the man born
blind in chapter 9 denotes that by His word the Lord is the light
of the world; the resurrection of Lazarus (chapter 11) points out
that He is "the resurrection and the life" to everyone who believes
in Him. The wonderful multiplication of the loaves (chapter 6)
prepares us for the discourse on Jesus as the true bread of life.
And we may suspect that in other places where the symbolic
signification is not indicated so clearly we are justified in seeking
such a sense, even though at times it may not be easy to discover
it, as for instance in the account of the miracle of the wine at
Cana, which John says is the first of Jesus' signs (2:11).

The other important mode of construction of his symbolism is found not in events, but in words. They are mostly the expressions of the Master, in which He points to Himself as the salvation of the world. They are the words of those great and impressive *symbols-of-salvation.* "I am the bread of life" (6:35). "I am the light of the world. He who follows me does not walk in the darkness, but will have the light of life" (8:12; cf. 1:5, 9; 9:5). "I am the door of the sheep. I am the good shepherd" (10:7, 9, 11). "I am the true vine" (15:1). "He, however, who drinks of the water that I will give him shall never thirst" (4:14; cf. 7:37-39).

All these sayings have the following points in common. First, they are self-revelations by Jesus, introduced by that deliberate *ego eimi,* "I am," which reminds us of the voice of God in the Old Testament. Secondly, all of them either state or imply the great and unique condition of faith: Jesus is the salvation of whoever believes. *Au fond,* all of them have the same signification, though with a different imagery, and for this reason the images are interchangeable, as is evident from 6:35: "I am the bread of life. He who comes to Me shall not *hunger,* and he who believes in Me shall never *thirst."* They make a strong appeal to a man's desire for happiness, to his need for security, in short, to his desire for life. Bread and water signify necessary foodstuffs, and thus life ("bread of life," "living water"); the vine represents the joy of life; the shepherd is the guide to life; the light of the world points out the way and gives assurance of avoiding darkness and death by the light of self-knowledge which enables one to reach his goal. All of them signify the one great good, the only good, life. These symbols are meaningful to everyone; they have universal human appeal, as has just been pointed out. At the same time, and this is typical of the realistic idealism of the evangelist, they were, all of them, concrete representations with a determined, historical meaning.

We would be led too far afield were we to prove this of each one individually. Let it suffice to refer to the "bread of life" of chapter 6, which is an ancient and universal image, but which because of its context here acquires an immediately historical sense that has relationship to the manna of the Exodus and to the figure of Moses, the first savior of the people of God. Further, it must be added that in later Judaism, whether that of the Palestinian rabbi or the Alexandrian philosopher, manna was not merely an erudite recollection of the past, but it had become a living religious symbol, an expression of their great expectation. Note that in these words Jesus is not compared with bread, or light, etc., but is identified with all of them, and that distinctively. He is not like the light, but He *is* the light, and even the *true* light, the true bread, the true vine, the good shepherd. He is the only savior, and He alone is savior. Although we do not wish to consider St. John a Platonist, it could be said that to him the visible world is but a reflection of what he calls the "truth," the divine reality which has assumed flesh in Jesus. What we call bread is only figuratively so, since it satisfies our hunger only for a time. The religious leaders who seek followers in isolation from Jesus are really "thieves" and "robbers" (10:8). The life which we seek separately from the Lord, is really not life—"What is existence that does not continue, but a flame that sinks into ashes?" (Marsman). The death which we fear is not death: "I am the resurrection and the life; he who believes in Me, even if he die, shall live; and whoever lives and believes in Me, shall never die" (11:25-26).

Typical of Johannine piety is the role assumed in the fourth Gospel by the sacraments of baptism and the Eucharist. True, he speaks of them explicitly in only a few passages (3:1 ff. and 6:51b-58), and it is to be noted that he does not record the institution of the Eucharist although he dedicates several chapters to the events and discourses of the Last Supper. We observe that for one reason or another he maintains a marked reserve on this point. And we notice his anxiety, as will become more evident, to locate the sacraments in the context to which they belong, among the great relationships formed by his ideas on the Spirit and on Christ as the heavenly Redeemer.

On the other hand, however, the words of the Lord on both

baptism and the Eucharist are almost of a crass realism: "Amen,
amen, I say to thee, unless a man be born again, he cannot see
the kingdom of God. . . . Unless a man be born again of water
and the Spirit, he cannot enter into the kingdom of God" (3:3,
5). "Amen, amen, I say to you, unless you eat the flesh of the Son
of Man, and drink His blood, you shall not have life in you. . . .
For My flesh is food indeed, and My blood is drink indeed"
(6:54, 56). We are not surprised that the words on the Eucharist
were a source of scandal not only to the unbelievers, but even to
the disciples (6:61, 66). Furthermore, these words about eating
His flesh and drinking His blood were no more acceptable to the
true Gnostic with his aversion for the material than they were to
His first hearers. But the circumstances and the context of chapter
6 afford the evangelist the opportunity of taking up the theme in
a framework where on the one hand there is still time for "decision" and for grumbling "scandal," [2] and on the other, the
Eucharistic pronouncements of the Master, in spite of their unmistakable realism, are linked with the words on Jesus as the
revealer and on the Spirit.

Verses 61–63 are clear enough on this point: "Does this scan-
dalize you? What then if you should see the Son of Man ascending
where He was before? It is the spirit that gives life; the flesh
profits nothing. The words that I have spoken to you are spirit
and life." Following on the strong formulas of verses 51–58, they
offer the reader a spiritualization which does not remove the
reality of the sacrament or vaporize it into a purely spiritual
"sharing by faith," but emphasizes the necessary interdependence
of sacrament and faith, of flesh and spirit. They point to the
mysteries of Jesus' heavenly origin and return, and to the life-
giving power of the Spirit. Thus, a misunderstanding which
would conceive the sacramental element to be only a material
rite, becomes impossible. Furthermore, in this manner the sacramental element is placed within the whole of the mystery of
salvation.

[2] Quite unlike chapter 13 and those that follow.

The sermon about the Lord as the bread of life (vv. 32–50), which precedes the Eucharistic passage, has the same intent. Jesus, who brings revelation, who is the true manna come from heaven, the second and perfect Moses, is by His word the "bread of life." This image, as has already been pointed out, indicates the totality of salvation which Jesus offers and which He Himself is, in which man is able to share by faith. It is under this universal dimension that the Eucharist is then introduced: "And the bread that I will give is My flesh for the life of the world" (v. 51b). The eating and drinking of Jesus' flesh and blood is a very distinctive and even necessary (v. 54) means by which the believer is nourished by the Lord as the bread of life. Only believers in the full sense of the term are able to grasp this.

Baptism as a rebirth from water and Spirit is similarly incorporated into the same large context of faith in the Lord and divine activity. In 20:21–23 we read how Jesus on the evening of the day of His resurrection appeared to the disciples and said: " 'Peace be to you! As the Father has sent Me, I also send you.' When He had said this, He breathed upon them and said, 'Receive the Holy Spirit; whose sins you shall forgive, they are forgiven them; and whose sins you shall retain, they are retained.' " Here, too, we have the same discretion coupled with clarity; here, too, the close association of the glorified Christ and the Spirit.

Thus, by the manner in which he transmits the sayings of the Lord on the sacraments, the evangelist remains true to the grandiose vision which animates his entire work, and signifies complete victory over the Gnostic attitude. With the incarnation of the Logos, eternal salvation, which had been prepared for and outlined by the Old Covenant, is definitively bound up with human time and human history. It is now inseparably tied up with bodily and material creation. In Christianity there is no room for an idealistic escape from matter. But the flesh "profits nothing" when it is separated from the life-giving Spirit. Creation is redeemed by its relationship to Christ, and through its reference to the Word is caught up even unto His glory. In our times, when throughout the Church a high respect for sacramental reality has happily emerged, when outside her pale can be seen new traces of reviving Gnosticism, these great ideas of the fourth Gospel afford the source for fruitful reflection. Our Christian insight is bound to grow, and our appreciation for these sacred symbols can only increase.

FIFTEEN

Again: Faith and Love

THE SPIRITUALITY of the fourth Gospel exists entirely in personal relationship to Christ and in "having the Son"; for whoever has the Son, has life, the only true life, the life which is "eternal." The problem of the possibility of Christian existence is then reduced to the problem of the possibility of this relationship to Jesus. How can a real and living bond arise between the Lord and the man who has never seen Jesus? This is one of the important questions which set the background for the Gospel and the first epistle. John wrote for a generation which had never met the Lord here on earth, for readers who, for the greatest part surely, did not belong to the Palestinian milieu which was the scene of Jesus' activity. How could they, and how can we, acquire relationship with Him who is the life, the way, and the truth? The answer of the fourth Gospel is that this is possible through faith in Christ and love for all the brothers and sisters in the Lord. This faith and this love do not exist in a purely idealistic and abstract realm; they cannot be separated from the historical existence of Him who became man. Even after the ascension, all Christian generations are linked with the earthly revelation of the glory of God which has taken place in Jesus.

It is the peculiar genius of the evangelist to be able to develop a subtle plot with simple words. Direct relationship to Christ begins by *faith*. John repeats endlessly: faith in Jesus, faith in His name, faith that He is, etc. But he also speaks about seeing and contemplating Christ, and about knowing Christ. Some insight into the interconnections between these three ways of understanding is indispensable for grasping his purport. The easiest approach is a short review of the ways he applies the different Greek verbs meaning "to see" to the notion of viewing Christ.[1]

First there is a merely empirical seeing of Jesus, which has no connection with faith and really is no seeing at all, but rather a blindness, as Jesus says to the unbelieving Jewish leaders who, together with His own disciples, had been eye-witnesses of His deeds: "For judgment have I come into this world, that they who do not see may see, and they who see may become blind" (9:39). Secondly, there is also a different kind of seeing on the part of the eye-witnesses. This is accompanied by faith and therefore sees in the scandal of the "flesh" the "glory" of the Only-begotten. "And the Word was made flesh, and dwelt among us. And we saw His glory—glory as of the only-begotten of the Father—full of grace and of truth" (1:14). This is put forth even more clearly in the introduction to the first epistle, where an appeal is made to all the senses to witness to the corporeal reality of the Logos: "I write of what was from the beginning, what we have heard, what we have seen with our eyes, what we have looked upon and our hands have handled: of the Word of Life. . . . What we have seen and have heard we announce to you, in order that you also may have fellowship with us" (1:1-3). This is seeing as both witnessing and believing taken together. This was the privilege of the contemporaries of the Lord, of the disciples who had been called to come forward as authentic witnesses. And it was they who were able to recognize the "sign" in His miracles. Thirdly there is faith, which is *contrasted* with bodily seeing and is pronounced blessed. Jesus said to Thomas: "Because thou hast seen Me, dost thou believe? Blessed are they who have not seen, and yet have believed" (20:29).

It is not without reason that this pericope about Thomas, who could not believe without seeing and touching, is used as the con-

[1] See O. Cullmann, *Urchristentum und Gottesdienst,* Zurich, 1950, pp. 39–60.

clusion of the fourth Gospel,[2] thus ending the whole with a most exalted confession in the Lord: "Thomas answered and said to Him, 'My Lord and my God!'" The evangelist is evidently appealing here to the faith of that later generation for which he is writing, and which had not seen. To arouse and deepen this faith is really the sole reason for writing his book (20:30–31).

This faith, however, *our* faith—which in a certain sense is the crowning of the whole Gospel and of the whole Scriptures and is not connected with a direct, personal seeing of the Lord— may not be regarded as a purely spiritual vision. It is this too; and if you will, it is such principally. Faith is aroused deep within us by God Himself. "No one can come to Me unless the Father who sent Me draw him, and I will raise him up on the last day. It is written in the prophets, 'And they all shall be taught of God.' Everyone who has listened to the Father, and has learned, comes to Me" (6:44–45).[3] This faith is spiritual insight: "Now this is everlasting life, that they may know Thee, the only true God, and Him whom Thou hast sent" (17:3; see 14:7–9, etc.). But it is always connected with and joined to the bodily vision of the One-who-became-flesh, so that in this point, too, we come across the polarity of spirit and flesh of which we spoke in the preceding chapter, and is so distinctive of the fourth Gospel. As is evident from the texts that have been quoted above (1:14; I John 1:1–3), our faith rests upon the actual seeing of eye-witnesses, on their testimony which continues in the preaching of the Church. And we may add here entirely in the spirit of John that our faith, too, goes hand in hand with a bodily contemplation of the divine glory in the form of flesh; for in the celebration of the liturgy and in

[2] Chapter 21 is really an appendix, as is apparent from the epilogue of 20:30–31.

[3] In characteristic fashion this text continues as follows: "not that anyone has seen the Father except Him who is from God (i.e., Jesus Himself), He has seen the Father." Contemplation, that is, direct knowledge of God is reserved for the next life; see I John 3:2 "We shall see Him as He is." This is the true blessedness of salvation, and we may consider this (strictly) eschatological seeing of God (in Christ) as the fourth way of knowing God, when added to the three already mentioned above.

the experience of the sacraments we see and hear and touch with faith, as did the apostles.

Linguistic statistics generally have interest only for specialists. But perhaps it will be of some import to others to know that the verb "to believe" occurs almost a hundred times[4] in the fourth Gospel, three-fourths of which occur in the first twelve chapters, which are dedicated to the revelation of Jesus to the world and the judgment of the world. For John, just as for Paul, the act of faith is a decision by which a person decides in favor of God who has revealed himself in Jesus, and thus escapes the judgment which has already been pronounced on the world. Whoever refuses to believe simply adds this condemnation to his own imputability; he is already condemned and need not wait for the "final" judgment (3:18, 36, etc.).[5]

One of the most distinctive features of Johannine thought consists in what may be called his anticipation of eschatology. He assures the Christians who toward the end of the first century were still anxiously looking for the Parousia—on this state of mind see the second epistle of Peter—that even before the second coming we may rightly speak of judgment, and that the believer will possess eternal life before the final resurrection. The decision, which involves both a discernment of spirits and a judgment, is a matter of the present. John has all this in mind with his word *krisis*. For him, as well as for the Apostle of the Gentiles, faith is the distinctive mark of the Christian life even *after* conversion. "You believe in God, believe also in Me," Jesus told His disciples

---

[4] Ninety-seven times, to be exact. At the same time it is most strange that the substantive *faith* is entirely lacking. A similar phenomenon can be noted with the words "to know" and "knowledge." Whereas the verb forms for "knowing" are used very frequently, the substantive *gnosis* (knowledge) is not used at all, not even in the epistles. However, this is readily understandable, once we realize that the evangelist wants to avoid the term because of its pejorative connotation.

[5] This must naturally not be considered an irrevocable judgment. True to his own mannerism, John speaks about an absolute and essential attitude of spirit. Whoever with full knowledge and deliberation actually rejects grace and persists in this attitude "is already judged."

in His farewell address (14:1). In Christianity, faith in God and faith in Jesus are on equal level. In the fourth Gospel we have left deism behind more than at any other time. John declares categorically: "No one has at any time seen God. The only-begotten Son, who is in the bosom of the Father, He has revealed Him" (1:18).

Whatever the Christian believes, therefore, has reference only to the Son; He is the essential object of our *Credo*. The disciple believes that Jesus is the Holy One of God (6:69), the Christ, the Son of God, who came into the world (11:27; 20:31, etc.); that God sent Him, that He is in the Father and the Father in Him (14:10), in one word: *that He is* (8:24; 13:19). This is repeated with an impressive monotony; and this is really the sole content of Jesus' preaching in the fourth Gospel, namely that God speaks to us through Him, through His words and through His "deeds," that He is the one who brings revelation and at the same time *is* Himself the revelation in the most literal sense of the term. For this reason Johannine faith, as well as that of Paul, includes personal relationship to the Lord. One cannot believe in His message without believing in Him. One cannot believe His words, one cannot believe that all He says is true without accepting Him wholly, without having trust in Him, without embracing Him and subjecting oneself to Him with loving surrender, for He himself is the message. He is wholly present in His word and in His deeds, which themselves are "words" (see 14:10). This is what John calls "believing in His name," accepting Him for everything He claims to be, "receiving" Him (1:12) such as He is. For this reason everyone who believes, has eternal life, even now.

The Johannine doctrine on love, agreeing essentially with the other books of the New Testament, is outstanding in three aspects: its absolute character, its strong emphasis on fraternal charity, and its censure of every indiscreet "exercise of love toward God." Concerning the last we have already remarked earlier that Paul almost never speaks about loving God. John goes much farther on this point. It would seem that in his first epistle he wants to warn against illusions of a (false) mystical love for God. Notwithstanding the avoidance of the word "gnosis," one nevertheless gets to hear about the marks of the true Gnostic throughout the entire epistle. The writer carries on a silent but positive and direct polemic by means of what may be called phrases of definition or of description which mark the style of this letter: "He who says that he knows Him, and does not keep His commandments, is a liar" (2:4). "He who knows God, listens to us" (4:6). The criteria of real gnosis and true love for God are faith in the incarnation and active fraternal charity. "For this is the love of God, that we keep His commandments; . . . and this is His commandment" —in the singular!—"that we should believe in the name of His Son Jesus Christ, and love one another, even as He gave us commandment" (5:3 and 3:23).

The necessary interconnection between these two ways of Christian life is indicated nowhere more clearly than in this passage of the first epistle: "If anyone says, 'I love God,' and hates his brother, he is a liar. For how can he who does not love his brother, whom he sees, love God, whom he does not see? And this commandment we have from Him, that he who loves God should love his brother also" (4:20-21). John therefore unquestionably acknowledges the possibility of a real love of the Christian for God, but he is not so effusive on the point as is our devotional literature, which seems to insist on placing constantly on our lips the most ardent aspirations of the saints. John always adds the commandments in the same breath, and it is always the Johannine commandments of faith and brotherly love which give reality to and incarnate the love of God which would otherwise appear so immaterial. The faith which he has in mind is specifically faith in the true incarnation of the Lord (I John 4:2; 5:5-6; II John 7); and his fraternal charity is one of action and reality (I John 3:18) toward one whom we "see," which means toward one who belongs to our human world, which cannot be idealized.

A Christian must not want to be in heaven before his time, but must remain a man among men. John will have no part in a love which wants to go directly to God without dealing with the incarnate Logos and the tangible, crass reality of human society. He rejects Gnostic spirituality, which reserves its love for immaterial, celestial essences: "To love the God of heaven and heavenly creatures means to tender them continuous respect. . . . Man is composed of a double nature so as to be able to answer to his twofold task, namely, of being in a state where he can simultaneously have a care for earthly things and love the divinity" (*Aesculapius,* 9). The Christian attitude toward man comprises more than "care"; it consists of a love which is directed toward another in his whole concrete reality.

For this reason the emphasis of John's preaching rests on brotherly love. It is more accurate to use this term rather than the expression "love of neighbor." The last is naturally not excluded from John's intention, but he speaks only of the mutual love of Christians. "He who loves his brother abides in the light" (I John 2:10). "For this is the message that you have heard from the beginning, that we should love one another" (3:11). And there are the words of the Master in the Gospel: "A new commandment I give you, that you love one another: that as I have loved you, you also love one another" (13:34). "This is My commandment, that you love one another as I have loved you" (15:12). The precept of love of neighbor is, as we have already seen in the other Gospels and in Paul, the summation of the "New Law" of Christianity. It is characteristic of John that he places the sayings of Jesus on brotherly love in the context of the farewell address, where the world is excluded and the traitor has departed (13:30–31); in the intimacy of Jesus' last stay "with His own" (13:1). That the evangelist does not mention love for those who are outside or for enemies is not so much the result of a feeling of partiality as the consequence of an exalted and profound insight. It is also consistent with his view on the world, as we have already explained. The world John speaks of, when thought out thoroughly to its last implication—as John loves to do—is an obstinate refusal to believe in Jesus, and *as such* it can have no share in true love. This apparent exclusiveness, however, is primarily a consequence of his sublime idea of *agape,* which both in origin and in intrinsic nature surpasses the purely psychological and even moral level. It is not only a gift of God, it is a sharing in God's own being. Whoever excludes himself from the fellowship with God, which has been offered us in the self-revelation of the Word, simply cannot receive it. *This* love is simply inconceivable without the notion of reciprocity; whoever rejects the Son toward whom the Father's love is primarily directed (3:35, etc.) cannot possibly be the object of *agape* in the full sense of the term.

In the preceding part we have already shown wherein lies the fullness of John's notion on love. Here we can do no better than transcribe I John 4:7–21: "Beloved, let us love one another, for love is from God. And everyone who loves is born of God and knows God. He who does not love does not know God; for God is love. In this has the love of God been shown in our case, that God has sent His only-begotten Son into the world that we may live through Him. In this is the love, not that we have loved God, but that He has first loved us, and sent His Son a propitiation for our sins" (vv. 7–10; one must naturally read the whole passage). For John, as well as for Paul (see Rom. 3:21–26; 5:5–8; Eph. 5:1–2, etc.), the sending of the Son, which culminated in the death on the cross because of love, revealed to us *in actu* who God is and what we are to think of Him. Paul prefers to speak about the grace and mercy of God; John refers to love; but they both mean the same.

Jesus, dying on the cross so that the world might live,[6] is the incarnate and therefore revealed love of God. He shows us God's essence. "God *is* love," not as a state of self-contained quiet, but an overflowing, self-sharing life which communicates itself with the Son, and through Him with every man who is willing to believe in this revelation of love. We did not know this love of God before God showed it to us in Jesus (I John 3:16; 4:9–10).

---

[6] The evangelist does not distinguish the death on the cross from His glorification; the Son of Man who was raised on the cross is already the glorified one, who draws all things to Himself by His Spirit and condemns the unbelieving world with its rulers (cf. 3:14–15; 8:28; 12:31–33; 14:30; 16:11; 19:37).

The initiative belongs to God alone, from whom the *agape* descends via the Lord to man. And the love which is in God, reveals itself among Christians as brotherly love. The mutual love of Christians is more than a moral obligation; it is above all a sharing in the divine love, it is a mark of the new life (I John 3:14), of having been born of God (4:7) and of the true gnosis. But with all this sublimity, or better, because of this supernatural origin, it remains real and active. "He who has the goods of this world and sees his brother in need and closes his heart to him, how does the love of God abide in him?" (I John 3:17). It is the tangible manifestation to the world of what Christianity really is and intends to be. Without it, all preaching remains but an idle word, as the history of the Church has shown on innumerable occasions. "By this will all men know that you are My disciples, if you have love for one another" (13:35). It is the achievement which the Lord expects from His disciples (15:1–7), His last word, His testament, the unworldly peace which He left us (14:27).

Conclusion

Now THAT we have come to the end of our survey and are about to draw a few conclusions, it is fitting that we should first justify the selection of the topics we discussed and excuse ourselves for the omission of other themes. I have often marveled at the efforts of anthologists to justify their work in view of the unavoidable dissatisfaction of critics, who thereby substantiate their right to exist. Every choice is subjective, and to that extent justified if it is truly the adequate expression of a personality trying to understand its world and its time. Now it is true that this book does not treat directly with *belles-lettres,* and the spiritual unity of the New Testament seems larger than, to use an example, the unity of Dutch lyric poetry in the course of the centuries.[1] But the original bond between the books of the New Testament is less than their common inclusion in the canon and liturgical usage would lead us to suspect. The literary relationship of the Pauline epistles to the Gospels is minimal. Furthermore, Paul's epistles are letters of occasion, at times fragmentary, often extremely meaningful, but never complete tracts. Even Romans, which most resembles a treatise, is not at all comparable to a theological handbook. The three oldest Gospels, in spite of their manifold differences, do present a remarkable uniformity. We treated them as

[1] Father Grossouw is a native of the Netherlands, and so naturally will refer to his own literature. (Trans.)

a unit, because this served our purpose, considering the Lord's sayings. But John's Gospel has an entirely unique character, distinguishing it sharply both from the Synoptics and from Paul, although among all these writings there are many evident as well as hidden traces of similarity, of which a few have been pointed out or explained in the preceding chapters. It was therefore necessary to make a choice here, too, in order to discover an appealing and meaningful design in this rich variety.

The nature of this selection was determined more by the importance which the New Testament itself attributes to some ideas than by the pertinence of these ideas for our day, although their practical usefulness was constantly kept in mind. Looked at in this way, the spirituality of the New Testament does not coincide completely with the Catholic piety of the present moment. Such an absolute identification would be utterly impossible; that it is not indispensable and not even desirable according to our Catholic doctrine has already been explained. However, there is need for constant recourse to the Scriptures in all ages and in every culture, in order to find both orientation and true perspective for our spiritual life in accordance with God's written word. It is in this spirit that we tried to sketch a simple yet lucid picture of the leading thoughts of the New Testament which touch on godliness.

That no mention was made here of the veneration of the Mother of God—to mention just one important example of the topics that were not discussed—which plays such a prominent role in modern piety, is thus explained by the principle we adopted for our choice. Even in the Scriptures themselves this veneration does not have the emphasis which it has received from tradition and devotion in the course of the centuries. This does not mean that the devotion of later centuries is bereft of biblical foundation. The manner in which Luke writes of Mary in the infancy narrative manifests an unmistakably deep veneration; she is portrayed with the features of the noble women of Israel's past, the mothers of God's people, even as she is in herself the personification of God's people, "the daughter of Sion" and the Ark of the Covenant.

In the fourth Gospel she appears but twice, with the epithet "the mother of Jesus"; once at the beginning of Jesus' public life at the wedding of Cana, and again at the end, when, before His death, the Master entrusts her to His beloved disciple. In both instances her function is as mysterious as it is meaningful. Although it is difficult to ascertain the full intent of the evangelist, this much is certain at least: that he associates her with the "hour" of Jesus' redemption and glorification as also with the community of the disciples, the Church. These two sketches of the figure of the Mother of God, which far exceed any historical records, are full of suggestion—they are not self-contained but open, turned toward the future, and one may rightfully assert that their full meaning was unveiled only in later times. But they play no further part in the words of Jesus or in the preaching of the apostles so far as these have been recorded in the New Testament.

Another omission, equally serious, of which the writer has been aware from the very beginning, and which has become more pronounced every time this work is reprinted, has to do with the doctrine of the New Testament on *prayer* and *liturgy*. Not that these topics have been entirely ignored in the preceding pages. They were always present, at least in the background, in the chapters on the Synoptic notion of God and the Pauline notion of faith. Something was also said about the prayer of supplication as found in the Gospels (pp. 81–83) and on the meaningful intimations of the fourth Gospel concerning the sacraments (pp. 171–178). But these limited references do not suffice to suggest even approximately the wealth of the New Testament on these matters. Much more attention ought really be given the sayings of Jesus on prayer, which Matthew has carefully collected, in His Sermon on the Mount (6:5–15), and the picture which Luke has drawn of the Master praying in solitude at night (see 3:21; 5:16; 6:12; 9:29; 10:21; 11:1; 22:32, 42; 23:34, 46). The same is true of the prayer of the first Christians, which is so attractive to us because of its simplicity and originality and about which the Acts of the Apostles give us sparing but enlightening details (see 1:24–25; 2:42, 46–47; 4:24–31; 6:4–6; 7:59–60; 9:11; 12:5; 13:3;

16:25, etc.). The epistles of the apostles, particularly those of St. Paul, afford much material on this point. Paul opens all his epistles by proclaiming his constant prayer and petition for the faithful to whom he is writing. Furthermore, quite frequently he gives the form and content of these prayers. Thus, the epistle to the Ephesians provides several examples of profound and exalted prayer in which we can at the same time see a reflection of mature Christian conduct (1:15–23; 3:13–19, followed by the strikingly beautiful doxology of 3:20–21). In the first letter to the Corinthians we are given all sorts of information on the meetings of that community, the celebration and primitive understanding of the Eucharist, the charisms, etc. Paul mentions the "psalms, hymns and spiritual songs" with which the first Christians sang to God and to each other, "making melody in their hearts" and "singing with the spirit" (Col. 3:16; Eph. 5:19; cf. I Cor. 14:15); and even transcribes a portion of one in Eph. 5:14 (see also I Tim. 3:16). And lastly there is the Apocalypse, with its snatches of heavenly liturgy, filled from first to last with glowing hymns of praise (4:8, 11; 5:9–13; 7:10–12; 11:17–18; 12:10–12; 15:3–4; 19:1–8).

There are yet other topics which ought to have more attention than just a passing reference; for instance, the Scripture's (i.e., the New Testament) own doctrine on veneration for the Scripture (i.e., the Old Testament) and how it is wholly inspired thereby; a theology of the word of God, of the apostolate, of suffering with Christ with the concomitant joy that is given by the Holy Spirit, and many others. But this must suffice, and it more than suffices, to note the incompleteness of this study, which was fully acknowledged in the Introduction itself.

In spite of its literary variations, the New Testament manifests an unmistakable unity. In all three "strata" which we have examined, we find the same message. The proper attitude of the Christian is, to put it as briefly as possible, faith in God and love for men. In the older Gospels Jesus speaks repeatedly about the two commandments, of confidence in God and of love for neighbor. It would be easy to compile from Paul's writings an anthology

of both dogmatic and poetic texts on faith in God who justifies
the impious and calls the dead to life; and we have seen how in
the world of human relationships he gave an all-encompassing
significance to love. And finally, the fourth Gospel is directed
entirely toward faith in God's Son, and the old and the new commandment which John repeats constantly is once again that of
agape. We ascertained further that faith according to the Scriptures
involves a personal relationship and can therefore stand for the
total surrender of the Christian to God.

The Christian's sentiment toward God is mostly called faith
by Paul and John, and seldom love. But it would be wrong to
think that the two are in opposition to each other. Rather, they
include each other; true faith in God implies love, and the latter
presupposes faith. The apostolic preference for faith as a description of one's relationship to God can be explained, it seems to me,
by their recognition of man's total dependence on God's grace,
which is automatically included in the New Testament concept of
"faith," but is not necessarily contained in the notion of love for
God. This is certainly true of Paul, and it has already been explained why John is critical about manifestations of love for God.

In the second place, it is clear that this fundamental attitude
may be called Christian only when faith and love are both con-
centrated on the person of Jesus Christ. In Him the kingdom of
God has come and is coming—the Synoptics. In the cross of Jesus
the grace of the merciful God has been made known and fully
actualized—Paul. Christ is the one who brings revelation and is
Himself the revelation—John. In Him our salvation has become
incarnate and is therefore both human and divine, definite in
history and universal in import. Because Christian piety fully
acknowledges this reality, it is not merely a religious attitude, but
an absolute reality which has become incarnate through faith in
the Church and love for existent man, by accepting the corporeal
and the whole of the creation. It is Christian by following Christ
in His struggle against sin and in His love for the sinner. It witnesses to Christ by a profession of His name, which goes hand in
hand with evangelical self-denial and renunciation. It acknowl-

edges sin in the Pauline sense of the term, and the necessity of mortification in order to overcome our inherent self-seeking.

Faith and love, when given Christian reality, imply Christian solidarity in the fellowship of Christ's body, the Church, which, though erected on its unique and God-given foundation, remains essentially directed to the totality of the human race. Possibly the most difficult problem for the typically modern man, who is so deeply convinced of his solitude and the absolute uniqueness of his existential experience, is to understand that his own life and death are simultaneously the life and death of the first man, Adam, and of the New Man, Christ. Faith in Jesus can overcome even the world of individualism with its inducement to despair; and love for neighbor gives us, *in Christ,* the possibility of a human society which shall always remain incomplete and broken in this life, but which contains the promise of the *societas perfecta sanctorum*— the perfect society of the saints.

Were one to reduce the spirituality of the New Testament to just one formula, it would have to read as follows: Faith in God and love for man, in the fellowship of Jesus Christ. And were one to point out in one phrase the most essential characteristic of Christian conduct, then it would be: Love of neighbor—in all the richness and variety it entails.

Scriptural References

DATE DUE

APR 1 5 1978		
NO 6 '83		
		PRINTED IN U.S.A.